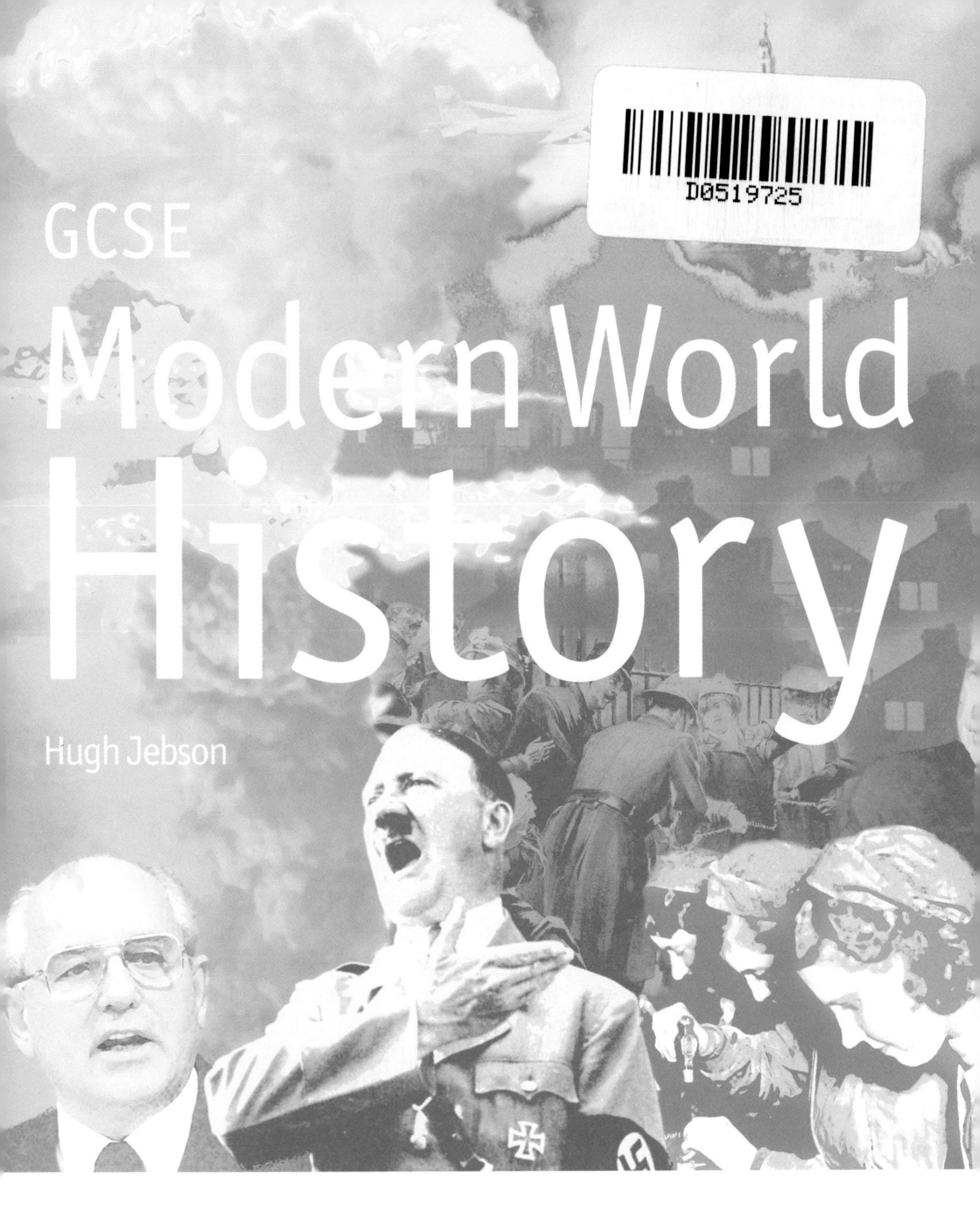

ESSENTIAL WORD

DICTIONARY

For Danelle, Alex, Aidan, Sophie, Mum and Dad

Philip Allan Updates, an imprint of Hodder Education, part of Hachette Livre UK, Market Place, Deddington, Oxfordshire OX15 0SE

Orders
Bookpoint Ltd, 130 Milton Park, Abingdon, Oxfordshire, OX14 4SB
tel: 01235 827720
fax: 01235 400454
e-mail: uk.orders@bookpoint.co.uk
Lines are open 9.00 a.m.–5.00 p.m., Monday to Saturday, with a 24-hour message answering service. You can also order through the Philip Allan Updates website: www.philipallan.co.uk

ISBN 978-0-86003-389-9

Acknowledgements
I am particularly grateful to Nicolas Kinloch for his thorough proofing and supportive comments.

Printed in Spain

P01383

Introduction

This *Essential Word Dictionary* contains over 400 historical terms that are used most often in GCSE modern world history.

Each entry is broken down into a maximum of three parts:

(1) The **headword** (in bold text) is followed by a simple definition.

(2) Further detail follows in the form of a series of bullet points to emphasise the entry in its historical context.

(3) An **examiner's tip** is then included where appropriate. The purpose of these tips is to enhance understanding of problematic terms and improve examination performance.

In many of the entries, one or more words are printed in *italics*. These are cross-references to words defined elsewhere in the dictionary. By cross-referencing to the words in italics, you will gain a fuller understanding of the entry you are reading.

The entries deal with the features of the core content (International Relations 1919–91) as well as the individual Depth Studies. Entries are included for the following Depth Studies and are identified by the icon DS:

- Germany 1918–45
- Russia 1905–70
- America 1919–70
- China 1945–90
- Britain 1900–51 (including the First World War)
- South Africa 1945–94
- Israel and the Arab Crisis 1945–94

Included in the dictionary are entries on:

- key historical figures
- major historical events such as wars and treaties
- important historical terms such as **armistice** and **authoritarianism**

The dictionary will help you in the following ways:

- to explain and understand a particular topic
- to define historical terms
- to highlight the significant names, places and events that are a common feature of the GCSE specification and examination
- as a revision aid

To use the dictionary as a revision aid, first compile a checklist of essential terms, events and individuals you need for an examination. Look these terms up in the dictionary and then learn and understand them so that you can use them with confidence in the examination.

The GCSE specification and examination require you to have considerable historical knowledge and to deploy this knowledge appropriately and selectively. Understanding the key terms in this dictionary will help you to do this. There is an element of luck with questions in all examinations, but you can increase the chance of having good luck in your GCSE history exams by knowing and understanding the key terms in this dictionary.

Abyssinian War, 1935–36: a conflict that followed the Italian invasion of the East African state of Abyssinia (Ethiopia).

- *Mussolini* wanted to create an empire modelled on ancient Rome. The Abyssinian leader, *Haile Selassie*, sought help from the *League of Nations* (1920–45), and the league condemned Italian aggression. In protest, Italy withdrew from the league. Other than censure Mussolini, the League of Nations did nothing to prevent the Italian conquest.
- The *Hoare–Laval Pact* (1935) was an attempt to appease Mussolini after Britain's and France's concerns about the growing threat of Nazi Germany. The proposed pact would have provided significant economic and territorial concessions to the Italians, but was so unpopular with the British and French people that it was withdrawn.

TIP The lack of a coherent international response to the Italian invasion demonstrated how Britain and France were linked to *appeasement* early on and revealed the flawed notion of *collective security*.

Acerbo Law: a component of *Mussolini's* consolidation of power in 1923, the Acerbo Law gave the party that won 25% of the votes in a national election two-thirds of the seats in the Italian parliament.

- The Acerbo Law paved the way for the April 1924 elections, during which the fascists used intimidation and ballot theft to secure the most parliamentary seats.
- Mussolini claimed the results demonstrated popular support for his party. A month after the election, the murder of Matteoti (the Italian socialist leader) secured Mussolini's hold on power.

TIP Mussolini justified the law by arguing that it would encourage stable and effective government in Italy, which had been absent in previous years.

Afghanistan, Soviet invasion of, 1979: an attempt by Moscow to strengthen *communism* in Afghanistan through military intervention.

- In 1979 Afghanistan was an unstable country; Muslim opposition groups attacked the pro-*Soviet* government of Hafizollah Amin and — with some 30 million Muslims in the *Soviet Union* — the leadership in Moscow was worried about Islamic militancy within its own borders.

- Control of Afghanistan would also put the Soviets closer to the Middle East and the oil reserves on which the US and its allies depended.
- Soviet forces ousted Amin and replaced him with Babrak Karmal. The communist government was opposed by Afghan rebels (*mujaheddin*) armed by Pakistan, the US and China. They fought a 10-year war before the Soviets withdrew.

TIP Soviet involvement in Afghanistan was the last chapter in the *Brezhnev Doctrine* and marked the end of *détente* as the US refused to ratify (support) SALT II, imposed economic sanctions on the Soviet Union and boycotted the 1980 Moscow Olympics.

DS **African National Congress (ANC):** a predominantly black organisation that fought to overturn the whites-only policies of the South African government.

- Formed in 1910 to unite African opinion, ANC members initially believed in passive resistance but became increasingly militant and violent after 1945.
- The ANC was banned in 1960 following the government massacre of peaceful protestors at Sharpeville. Its leader at the time was *Mandela*.
- Following years of international pressure, the government legalised the ANC in 1990.

TIP The ANC remained at the heart of the struggle against *apartheid*.

Agadir: a port city in Morocco that, in 1911, was at the centre of an international dispute involving France, Germany and Britain.

- At the end of the nineteenth century, Morocco was one of few African countries not colonised by the imperial powers. Its rich mineral and agricultural resources made it an inviting prospect, in particular to the German government.
- The Algeçiras Conference (1906) discussed the future of Morocco; other than Austria, no country supported German claims. France was accepted as caretaker of Morocco but soon began to colonise it.
- In 1911 the Germans sent the battleship *Panther* to Agadir as a show of force. The crisis ended when Germany was forced to back down because of strong British support for France.

TIP German bitterness towards Britain drove the two countries further apart, heightened international tension and strengthened the *Alliance system*.

DS **Agricultural Adjustment Agency (AAA), 1933:** one of the 'alphabet agencies' set up by President *Roosevelt* to deal with the economic problems facing the US during the 1930s.

- The AAA paid US farmers to produce less, the idea being that an adjustment in the amount of food grown would lead to greater profits. During the next 2 years,

farmers received $120 million of subsidies in return for taking some 10 million acres of land out of cotton production, 8 million acres out of wheat production and slaughtering some 6 million pigs.

- At a time when many in the USA's major cities were affected by hunger, the AAA was bound to be controversial. In 1936 the *Supreme Court* declared it illegal.

TIP Although the AAA raised agricultural prices and farmers' incomes, many smaller farmers lost out to the more established farms that received the bulk of government subsidies.

DS **Al Fatah:** a *guerrilla* organisation set up in 1957 to liberate *Palestine* from Israeli occupation.

- Al Fatah is part of the *Palestine Liberation Organisation* and was responsible for raids launched on Israeli villages, government buildings and military posts from bases in Syria, Jordan and Lebanon.
- Recruits to Fatah came from camps in Jordan that housed over 350,000 Palestinian refugees after 1967. Between then and 1970, Fatah raids killed over 500 Israelis. Other Fatah tactics included assassinations, plane hijackings and hostage taking.

TIP Attempts by *Arafat*, the Al Fatah leader, to resolve the conflict through moderation caused the organisation to splinter into several smaller armed groups, each violently opposed to negotiations with the Israelis.

Alliance system: a series of international agreements that were in place in Europe by 1914.

- Growing tension between European powers at the turn of the nineteenth century led to the creation of two separate political and military camps.
- The *Triple Alliance* joined Austria–Hungary and Germany with Italy and pitted them against the *Triple Entente* of Britain, Russia and France.
- These alliances were supposed to be defensive in nature and to come into effect only if one member was attacked first.

TIP The Alliance system created the political context for the way that the killing of Archduke *Franz Ferdinand* triggered a world war of unprecedented suffering.

Alsace and Lorraine: a province of northeastern France that was at the centre of Franco-German disputes from 1870 until 1945.

- Germany annexed the region in 1871. It was restored to the French by the Treaty of *Versailles* (1919), conquered once again in 1940 by Hitler and then finally liberated in 1945.

TIP Alsace–Lorraine's rich iron ore deposits added an economic dimension to its strategic importance.

DS **ANC:** see *African National Congress*.

DS **Andropov, Yuri:** leader of the *Soviet Union* (1982–84).

- Andropov was Soviet ambassador to Hungary during the *Hungarian Uprising* (1956) and played an important role in organising the *Red Army* to crush the rebels.
- From 1967 to 1982, Andropov headed the *KGB* and launched a successful campaign against corruption and inefficiency in industry.
- Andropov succeeded *Brezhnev* in 1982, but was in office only 15 months before he fell ill and died. His successor, Constantin Chernenko, lasted little more than a year before he too died. His replacement was *Gorbachev*.

TIP

Andropov introduced a series of moderate reforms that increased industrial output in the Soviet Union.

Anglo-German Naval Treaty, 1935: an agreement between Britain and Germany whereby the size of the German navy would reach 35% of the navies of the entire British Empire.

- The treaty was signed without first consulting France or Italy; it harmed Anglo-French relations and undermined attempts to build a unified front against Germany.

TIP

The Anglo-German Naval Treaty contributed to the collapse of the *Stresa Front* (1935) and moved Italy and Germany closer. In signing the treaty, the British government helped *Hitler* break the Treaty of *Versailles* (1919).

Anschluss, 1938: the forced annexation (takeover) of Austria by Germany.

- The Treaty of *Versailles* (1919) banned direct German involvement in Austria.
- An Austrian Nazi coup was foiled in 1934.
- Schuschnigg became chancellor after Austrian Nazis murdered *Dolfuss* in 1934.
- By 1938, the Austrian economy continued to suffer the aftermath of the *Wall Street Crash* (1929) and support for closer ties to the more prosperous Germany was high. *Hitler* therefore marched unopposed into his native country.
- The lack of international opposition encouraged Hitler to set his sights next on Czechoslovakia.
- Hitler achieved one of his major *foreign policy* aims, which was to unite the German-speaking peoples.

TIP

Britain and France did nothing to prevent Anschluss; at the time many felt the Treaty of Versailles was in need of revision. Furthermore, Italy was allied to Germany by the *Rome–Berlin Axis* (1936).

Anti-Comintern Pact, 1937: an agreement between Germany, Italy and Japan to stop the spread of *communism*.

TIP

By including Japan, *Hitler* extended the *Rome–Berlin Axis* (1936) and formed a military alliance between the three countries.

anti-Semitism: hostility towards the Jewish religion and Jews.

- The nineteenth and twentieth centuries witnessed a steady increase in violent anti-Semitism, particularly in Russia.

TIP The Nazi regime is most closely associated with anti-Semitism, with the *Final Solution* and the *Holocaust*.

DS **ANZAC:** the Australia and New Zealand Army Corps that fought with Britain during the *Great War* (1914–18).

- The ANZACs fought their biggest campaign at the Gallipoli peninsula (Dardanelles) in 1915. *Churchill*, the first lord of the admiralty, hatched the plan in the belief that a series of amphibious landings followed by a rapid advance on the capital, Constantinople (Istanbul), could knock Turkey out of the war.
- From its start, the campaign was a disaster; the Turks were dug in on high ground overlooking the landing areas and kept the attackers pinned down for 8 months before a withdrawal took place.
- Conditions at Gallipoli quickly deteriorated into a carbon copy of the *Western Front* — bloody stalemate and *trench warfare*.

DS **apartheid:** the South African government policy from 1948 to 1993 to divide South Africans into separate and segregated racial groups.

- A series of laws was put into effect to keep black South Africans as second class citizens in their own country. They were required to carry an identity card, or pass, and to produce it immediately when stopped by the police.
- The police responded to a peaceful protest against the Pass Laws at Sharpeville in 1960 with volleys of fire that left dozens dead.
- Protests against apartheid included an international boycott of South Africa from the 1970s to the 1990s.
- *Mandela's* election as president in 1994 led to the dismantling of apartheid in South Africa.

TIP From 1945 to 1993, apartheid remained the main issue affecting political developments within South Africa as well as international relations with the white government.

appeasement: the policy of giving in to at least some of the demands of an aggressor in the belief that this will help to avoid conflict.

- Appeasement was the cornerstone of British and French *foreign policy* towards Germany and Italy during the late 1930s.
- The British prime minister, *Chamberlain*, is seen by many as the embodiment of appeasement.
- Events reached a turning point at Munich in September 1938 when — without first consulting the Czechs — Chamberlain and the French leader, Daladier, handed *Hitler* the *Sudetenland*.
- In March 1939, Germany occupied the remainder of Czechoslovakia and the countdown to the *Second World War* (1939–45) began.

TIP British appeasement of Hitler actually began before Chamberlain with the *Baldwin* government (1935–37), and it remained popular with the majority of the British people right up to 1939.

DS **April Theses, 1917:** a document issued by *Lenin*, leader of the Bolshevik Party, immediately following his return to Russia from exile in Switzerland.

- The document contained Lenin's 10-point political programme, calling for an immediate end to Russian involvement in the *Great War* (1914–18), total withdrawal of support for the *Provisional Government*, transfer of political power to the workers' *soviets*, nationalisation of land and banks and the establishment of an international body to spread worldwide revolution.
- Hoping Lenin would spread unrest, the German government helped him return to Russia in 1917.

TIP The April Theses are important to understanding how the Bolsheviks came to power.

DS **Arab–Israeli Wars, 1948–73:** four relatively brief but intense conflicts fought between Israel and the Arab states.

- The first of the Arab–Israeli conflicts in 1948 started when Arab armies attacked from Jordan, Egypt, Syria and Saudi Arabia. They were poorly coordinated and badly led against a better-trained Israeli army that was backed by the resolve of a people who had no option but to fight to the bitter end. The war ended in 1949 with over a million Arabs fleeing from *Palestine* to live in refugee camps in neighbouring states.
- The second Arab–Israeli war in 1956 was linked to the *Suez Crisis* and sparked by a joint British, French and Israeli assault on Egypt. In October 1956, Israel attacked and occupied the *Gaza Strip*; peace was restored along the old Egypt–Israel border by *United Nations* troops.
- Israel began the *Six-Day War* in 1967 with a surprise attack on the main Arab military airfields. Operating according to the belief that attack is the best form of defence, the Israelis advanced across the *Sinai* into Jordan and captured the *Golan Heights* from Syria. Israel refused United Nations pleas for a return to old borders and instead occupied the *West Bank* as well as parts of the Sinai.
- A joint Egyptian–Syrian surprise attack on Israeli targets during a Jewish holy day started the Yom-Kippur War (1973). The Arab states' goal was to reclaim land lost during the 1967 conflict; they met, at first, with success until US aid — aircraft and artillery — arrived, and the Israelis drove the Arabs back. Again, the United Nations brokered a cease-fire, with the Israelis strengthening their hold in the Sinai and on the Golan Heights.

TIP Other than the territory returned by the *Camp David Agreement* (1978), all other land seized by Israel after 1967 remains under its occupation. Tension in the region continues to run high.

DS **Arab League:** an organisation formed in 1945 to strengthen economic and cultural links between Arab states.

- Because of its influence in the region, Britain was instrumental in setting up the league. The first members were Egypt, Syria, the Lebanon and Saudi Arabia. Several more Arab states joined after gaining independence; all are united in their opposition to Israel.

TIP The British intended the Arab League to hold back *Soviet* progress and influence in the Middle East during the *Cold War* (1945–91).

DS **Arafat, Yasser:** president of the *Palestine Liberation Organisation* since 1969.

- As a founder *Al Fatah*, Arafat was the Palestinian nationalist *guerrilla* who coordinated military activities of the various groups within the PLO with the aim of creating a democratic, non-religious and independent Palestinian state.
- In 1993, Arafat rejected the use of terrorism and recognised Israel's right to exist in peace and security. He and Israeli leader Yitzhak Rabin signed a peace agreement that saw Arafat become leader of the Palestinian territories on the *West Bank* and in *Gaza*.

TIP Arafat is central to understanding the Middle East crisis and ongoing Israeli–Palestinian conflict.

armistice: a cease-fire arranged between warring parties or countries while a permanent political settlement is being arranged.

- Fighting in the *Great War* (1914–18) ceased with the armistice signed on 11 November 1918.
- The conflict did not officially end until 28 June 1919, when Germany signed the Treaty of *Versailles*.

arms race: a continuous competition between rival countries or alliances to build stockpiles of weapons in order to secure a military advantage.

- Britain and Germany engaged in a naval arms race before 1914. A more recent example is the one between NATO and the *Warsaw Pact* during the *Cold War* (1945–91).

TIP The Cold War arms race led to stockpiling of atomic weapons by both sides; at one point enough were available to destroy the world population eight times over.

DS **Asquith, Herbert:** the Liberal prime minister (1908–16) who led Britain into the *Great War* (1914–18).

- Asquith was a Liberal MP who, before becoming prime minister, was home secretary and chancellor of the exchequer. Some of the issues he faced included the *suffragettes*, reform of the House of Lords, industrial strife and the threat of civil war in Ireland.
- On 4 August 1914, Asquith declared war on Germany. A year later he formed a *coalition government* to secure political solidarity in the face of growing disquiet

over the military stalemate and rising cost of the war. This was not enough to save him; the *Conservatives* and his successor, *Lloyd George*, removed him from office in 1916.

TIP

Asquith's time as prime minister marks a turning point in the fortunes of the *Liberal Party*. The in-fighting that followed his resignation left his party weak and divided, and the *Labour Party* replaced it as the alternative to the Conservatives.

Atlantic, Battle of the: a sea campaign waged continuously around the British Isles during the *Second World War* (1939–45).

- The sea routes around Britain were vital to the country's ability to fight the war. The most intense fighting took place between 1940 and 1943 when Allied shipping lanes were subject to German attacks from surface vessels, long-range aircraft and *U-boats*. Thousands of Allied merchant ships were sunk during this time with heavy loss of life.
- Allied measures to keep the flow of sea trade open included convoys of commercial vessels escorted by warships and aircraft carriers, land-based air cover, radar and Asdic, an underwater detection device.

TIP

Allied success in the Battle of the Atlantic prevented mass starvation in Britain and allowed the flow of men and materials necessary for ultimate victory.

Atlantic Charter: a statement of principles issued by *Churchill* and *Roosevelt* following their meeting in August 1941 on a British warship off the coast of Canada.

- The charter was a set of war aims similar to those of President *Wilson* in the First World War: collective security; self-determination; disarmament; economic cooperation; and freedom of the seas.
- The Atlantic Charter was signed before the US officially entered the European conflict, and it therefore signified that the US was at (undeclared) war against Germany.

TIP

The charter established a foundation for postwar international organisation; in January 1942, 26 nations signed the Declaration of the *United Nations* which promised active support and backing for the Atlantic Charter.

atomic bomb: a weapon of mass destruction that played a key role in ending the *Second World War* (1939–45) and overshadowed international relations during the *Cold War* (1945–91).

- Between 1939 and 1945, Allied and German scientists raced to develop a nuclear weapon; the first successful detonation took place in New Mexico on 17 July 1945.
- Three weeks later, on 6 August, the Japanese city of Hiroshima was the first to be attacked with a nuclear weapon; over 100,000 people were killed or seriously wounded.

- A second bomb on Nagasaki 3 days later killed tens of thousands more and persuaded the Japanese government formally to surrender on 14 August.

TIP Nuclear weapons changed the course of human history.

DS **Attlee, Clement:** the British Labour prime minister (1945–51) who oversaw the creation of the *welfare state*.

- Attlee served as a junior minister between 1930 and 1931 but broke with the *Labour Party* leader, *MacDonald*, when the *National Government* was formed. He became leader of the Labour Party in 1935 and entered *Churchill's* wartime *coalition* in 1940.
- Attlee was deputy prime minister from 1942 until the war ended. He became prime minister following Labour's victory in the 1945 general election and his government pledged to nationalise, or take over, Britain's main industries.
- Other significant events of Attlee's career include the manufacture of Britain's first *atomic bomb*, the full independence of India, the meeting with *Stalin* and *Truman* at *Potsdam* (1945) and the introduction of social and economic reforms in Britain.

DS **Auschwitz–Birkenau:** the largest and most terrible of the *death camps* where the Nazis murdered over 3 million people (mostly Jews) between 1942 and 1945.

- The death camp was built alongside the main railway junction outside the Polish town of Krakow and comprised prisoner barracks, factories where inmates worked, large gas chambers disguised as showers and industrial capacity crematoria.
- Upon arrival by train, prisoners were separated into two groups, those to be worked to death and those — typically young children and old people — to be killed immediately.
- Soviet soldiers liberated the camp in 1945. Its ruins stand today as a vivid reminder of the hatred and inhumanity of the Nazi regime.

autarky: a government policy of economic self-sufficiency — particularly in agriculture and industry — in order to be independent of foreign trade.

- Nationalist governments in Italy and Germany during the 1930s adopted autarky, so the threat of economic blockade by rival states could not deter them from carrying out their foreign policies.

authoritarianism: a political system in which the government rules the population through strict and forceful control.

- Authoritarianism demands obedience to the state and authoritarian regimes typically employ police and military forces to override the rights and freedoms of individual citizens.
- Power in an authoritarian regime usually lies in the hands of a small group of individuals.

TIP Germany, Italy and the *Soviet Union* are examples of countries that were governed by authoritarianism.

autocracy: a political system whereby an individual governs a country without legal restraint and is not answerable to any group or individual.

- Twentieth-century autocratic rulers include *Nicholas II* of Russia and *William II* of Germany.

autonomy: self-government or the freedom to act independently.

- Autonomous states are those which have full political independence and are not obliged to accept demands or decisions of any other authority.

TIP The pursuit of autonomy is a major feature of the post-1945 histories of many non-Western countries, particularly former colonies of the European powers.

axis: term given to a group of countries with mutually supportive foreign policies.

- *Mussolini* first introduced the term in 1936 to describe Italy's alliance with Germany through their respective capital cities, Rome and Berlin.

TIP The *Rome–Berlin Axis* (1936) became the *Tripartite Pact* in 1940 when Japan joined. These three countries fought as allies for much of the *Second World War* (1939–45).

balance of power: the means of trying to prevent a single state from becoming dominant.

- The search for a balance of power in Europe at the turn of the century led to the *Alliance system* that, in turn, contributed to the outbreak of the *Great War* (1914–18).

DS **Baldwin, Stanley:** British Conservative prime minister (1923–24, 1924–29 and 1935–37).

- Baldwin led the country during the *General Strike* (1926). His response to the strikers' grievances left a legacy of hostility between the Conservatives and the British *trade union* movement.
- In 1931 he was invited to serve in the *National Government* and became its leader 4 years later.
- Baldwin resigned in 1937 over a crisis involving the royal family. *Chamberlain* succeeded him.

TIP *Appeasement* was the cornerstone of British *foreign policy* during Baldwin's government.

DS **Balfour Declaration:** a statement issued in November 1917 by the British foreign secretary, Lord Balfour, outlining British support for the establishment of a Jewish national home in *Palestine*.

- The Balfour Declaration came about in part because the British believed that US Jews could influence their government to support Britain during the *Great War* (1914–18).
- Balfour also called for action to be taken so that 'nothing shall be done which may harm the civil and religious rights of existing non-Jewish communities in Palestine'.

TIP The declaration came at a time when the First World War was going badly for Britain, and this influenced Balfour's decision to publish it.

DS **Baltic States:** the Eastern Europe territories of Latvia, Lithuania and Estonia.

- These states won independence from Russia in 1918. Twenty-two years later

they were absorbed into the *Soviet Union*, and they remained under Moscow's control until 1990.

- With the collapse of the Soviet Union in 1991, the Baltic States once again won independence.

Barbarossa, Operation, 1941: the code name given to the German invasion of the *Soviet Union* that began on 22 June 1941.

- *Hitler's* hatred of *communism*, coupled with his desire for *Lebensraum*, made the Soviet Union Germany's most obvious target. Despite numerous warning signs, the invasion caught the Russians unprepared and the Germans quickly advanced to the outskirts of Moscow.
- Heavy resistance blocked the invasion. Russia's oldest ally — its weather — also played an important role when rain and freezing temperatures slowed the mechanised German advance.

TIP The Russo-German conflict (1941–45) remains the most costly in the history of warfare. Both sides suffered millions of military and civilian casualties.

battle for grain: a propaganda slogan used to describe *Mussolini's* attempt to solve Italy's economic problems between 1925 and 1939.

- This battle was fought to raise wheat production, so that Italy would not have to depend on foreign exports. While more wheat was grown, it was at a cost to other valuable goods such as fruit and dairy products.
- Other non-military 'battles' included: the battle for land to drain swamps and marshes; the battle for the lira, which aimed at restoring the value of the Italian currency; and the battle for births which rewarded couples with children and taxed bachelors and those without children. In 1933 Mussolini hosted a reception for Italian mothers with 14 or more children.

TIP Mussolini's domestic battles achieved propaganda success; but material success was limited.

Bay of Pigs, 1961: the site of an ill-fated invasion by 1,200 US-backed anti-*Castro* Cuban exiles.

- As the *Cold War* (1945–91) intensified, President *Kennedy* authorised the CIA to go ahead with a plan to overthrow the communist leader.
- The US believed a small landing in Cuba would lead to a popular uprising against Castro's government. It was a disastrous miscalculation because Cuban forces routed the poorly trained and ill-equipped attackers.

TIP Things could not have worked out worse for the US government. Castro's popularity with his people increased and he moved Cuba strongly towards *Khrushchev* for protection.

DS **Beer Hall Putsch, 1923:** *Hitler's* armed attempt to seize power in Munich as the first step towards overthrowing the *Weimar Republic* and installing *Ludendorff* as German leader.

- *Hyperinflation* and the French occupation of the *Ruhr* led to Hitler's mistaken confidence that the German people would support him against the democratic government.
- Local military and police refused to support Hitler and instead broke up his march on 8 November with gunfire. It left 16 Nazis dead and Hitler under arrest.
- Hitler was tried and convicted of treason and a sympathetic judge sentenced him to 5 years' imprisonment. Hitler served only 9 months in prison, during which time he wrote *Mein Kampf.*

TIP The failure of the *putsch* was a defining moment for Hitler's political career. It taught him that revolution would not be achieved through force alone. Instead he sought power through the ballot box and participated in the parliamentary process he despised.

DS **BEF:** see *British Expeditionary Force.*

Benes, Eduard: the Czechoslovakian president at the time of the *Munich Agreement* (1938).

- Confident of British and French backing, Benes was prepared to fight Germany over the *Sudetenland.* He resigned in protest at Anglo-French *appeasement.*
- Between 1941 and 1945, Benes headed the exiled Czechoslovak government in London. He returned to serve as his country's first postwar leader.
- Despite his increasingly pro-Russian views, Stalin distrusted Benes; he was forced out in 1948 and replaced by hard-liners who placed the country firmly behind the *Iron Curtain.*

DS **Ben Gurion, David:** a founder of Israel and its first prime minister.

- Ben Gurion served two terms (1948–53 and 1955–63), both dominated by wars against the Arab states.

Berlin Airlift, 1948–49: an Anglo-American strategy to break the *Soviet* blockade of West Berlin.

- The wartime allies fell out over the future of Germany; *Stalin* wanted it to remain weak and divided while the Western powers wanted to see it prosper.
- Berlin was a divided city in the Russian-controlled zone of a divided Germany. Disagreement over a new German currency led to the Soviet attempt to force out Britain, France and the US by blocking road and rail traffic.
- The Western powers broke the blockade by flying thousands of tons of supplies into West Berlin.
- The former allies came close to war with each other. However, the Russians were unwilling to shoot down Allied aircraft because Stalin did not want to risk war with the west when the US had the *atomic bomb* and he did not. Stalin called off the blockade on 12 May 1949.

TIP The episode caused a serious deterioration of relations and solidified the separation of East and West Germany.

Berlin Wall, 1961–89: a wall built in 1961 to separate East Berlin (the capital of the *German Democratic Republic*) from West Berlin.

- Armed guards, watchtowers, minefields and electric fences discouraged East Berliners from trying to cross to the west and many people were killed attempting to escape.
- The wall dividing Berlin was part of the *Iron Curtain* that divided Eastern and Western Europe from 1945 to the end of the *Cold War* (1945–91).

TIP The Berlin Wall remained the most powerful symbol of the Cold War. Throughout, it was at the heart of the conflict and continued to be a potential flashpoint for war between NATO and the *Warsaw Pact.*

DS **Beveridge Report, 1942:** a proposal for social reform that provided the blueprint for the British *welfare state.*

- Named after the head of the government-appointed committee to investigate social issues in Britain, the Beveridge Report identified 'five giants' to be overcome — want, disease, ignorance, squalor and idleness.
- The report argued that the state has a responsibility to provide its people with a minimum income and basic health care, housing and education.

TIP *Churchill* did not approve of the Beveridge Report, and it was left to the *Labour* government of 1945–51 to introduce a welfare state.

Big Three: the name given to the leaders of the Allied powers at the end of the *Great War* (1914–18) and the *Second World War* (1939–45) who were responsible for drawing up the postwar peace settlements.

- In 1919 the Big Three were *Wilson* (US), *Lloyd George* (Britain) and *Clemenceau* (France).
- At the end of the Second World War, the Big Three were *Truman* (US), *Churchill* and *Attlee* (Britain) and *Stalin* (USSR).

blackshirt: the uniform of the *Fasci di Comabettimento*, the *Mussolini* supporters who organised themselves into fighting groups.

- Blackshirts were the uniformed private army of the Italian Fascist Party and were infamous for their violence towards anti-fascists.

TIP Mussolini's use of the blackshirts to silence his opponents became a model for other extreme right-wing parties, including the German Nazis and the British Union of Fascists.

DS **Blitz:** the name given to the German air raids on Britain's main cities between August 1940 and June 1941.

- By targeting railways, factories, ports and houses, *Hitler* hoped to destroy Britain's ability and willingness to resist. Heavy raids destroyed the centres of Coventry, London, Bristol and Liverpool.
- The Blitz ended in the summer of 1941 when German bombers were relocated to the east in preparation for Operation *Barbarossa*. German bombing continued

throughout the war on a less intense scale and some 60,000 British civilians were killed between 1940 and 1945.

TIP The Blitz is closely linked to the Battle of *Britain* and the two events should be studied together.

blitzkrieg: 'lightning war', the tactic used by the German army to great success between 1939 and 1941.

- Interwar British and French military planners looked to the lessons of the *Great War* (1914–18). The Germans, however, revolutionised land warfare using a coordinated combination of armoured speed, mechanisation and air power.
- A blitzkrieg attack smashed through the enemy lines with great speed in order to avoid a long, drawn out conflict.

TIP The tactic of overwhelming and sudden attack was a major factor in Germany's rapid victories over Poland and France, as well as its early success against the *Soviet Union*.

DS **Bolshevik:** see *Bolshevism*.

DS **Bolshevism:** a revolutionary movement that was the forerunner of the Russian Communist Party.

- The Social Democratic Party split in 1903 over leadership and policy differences. Two factions emerged — the Bolsheviks (or majority) and *Mensheviks* (or minority).
- While both factions believed in creating a socialist state in Russia, they differed on how to get there. The Bolsheviks were more radical, believing that only a small, dedicated band of full-time revolutionaries could overthrow the regime. The more moderate Mensheviks sought a wider power base.
- Vladimir Ulyanov, or *Lenin*, was leader of the Bolsheviks.
- The Bolshevik *October Revolution of 1917* led to the creation of the *Soviet Union*.

TIP Bolshevism's political success was due largely to the great organisational skills of Lenin and the changes he brought to the party.

boom: a period of economic prosperity.

- Rising wages, increased trade, and higher employment, profits and prices are all characteristics of a boom.
- During the 1920s, the US economy experienced a boom that was the envy of the world.

TIP A boom is often followed by a *depression*. The two events should be looked at together.

DS **bootlegger:** an individual who transported and sold re-distilled alcohol during *Prohibition* in the US during the 1920s.

- Prohibition banned production of alcohol, and so the type of illicit alcohol a

bootlegger sold was often intended for use in paint and cosmetics and could prove fatal if consumed.

TIP Bootleggers were a key feature of the Prohibition era and are closely associated with homemade alcohol called moonshine that was sold in illegal drinking establishments called speakeasies.

Bosnia–Herzegovina: a region of the former Yugoslavia that became an independent republic in 1992.

- Before 1918, the Austrians governed Bosnia. *Franz Ferdinand*, the heir to the Austrian throne, was assassinated in Sarajevo, capital of Bosnia, in 1914. Following the Austrian defeat in the *Great War* (1914–18), Bosnia became part of the new state of Yugoslavia.
- In 1992 Bosnia followed the example of Croatia and Slovenia (the other Yugoslav breakaway provinces) and declared its independence. A civil war followed that had significant religious as well as political overtones; predominantly Muslim Bosnia fought against largely Christian Serbia. The war ended in 1995.

TIP Recent Bosnian history is associated with ethnic cleansing — the intimidation and murder of civilians and the creation of refugee populations.

Brest–Litovsk, Treaty of, 1918: a peace treaty between Germany and Russia that was signed by *Lenin*.

- Russian involvement in the *Great War* (1914–18) brought about unprecedented political, economic and military disaster.
- Russia's losses in the treaty were severe: 74% of its iron ore and coal, 26% of its railways, 26% of its entire population, and 27% of its farmland. In addition, Germany charged Russia a war indemnity of 300 million roubles.
- With the war's outcome still in the balance in 1917, the allies pressed Lenin to fight on. When *Trotsky* — Lenin's representative at the peace talks — saw the German terms, he advised Lenin to do what the allies wanted. Regardless, Lenin wanted Russia out of the war and saw peace at any price as the best way to secure a Bolshevik victory.
- Britain and the US subsequently sent supplies and men to help the *White Russians* during the Russian Civil War (1918–21). The roots of the *Cold War* (1945–91) can be traced to this failed Western policy.

TIP Germany's treatment of Russia is seen as a clear indication of how it would have dealt with a defeated France and Britain. This is important to remember when deciding whether or not the Treaty of *Versailles* (1919) was too harsh on Germany.

DS **Brezhnev, Leonid:** leader of the *Soviet Union* (1964–82).

- Brezhnev became first secretary of the Communist Party when economic and *foreign policy* failures forced *Khrushchev* to resign.

- At home he cracked down on opponents of his policies. Like his predecessor, Brezhnev was unable to overcome many of his country's basic economic problems.
- The *Brezhnev Doctrine* and, later on, *détente* towards the US guided his foreign policy. In 1979, he sent the *Red Army* into *Afghanistan* in support of a communist government there.

TIP Brezhnev dominated Russian politics for almost 20 years and is an important figure in the *Cold War* (1945–91).

Brezhnev Doctrine: it stated that any communist country was obliged to intervene directly — with force, if necessary — to prevent any other communist country falling to *capitalism*.
- *Brezhnev* had been greatly shaken by the *Hungarian Uprising* (1956) and this informed his belligerence in international affairs.
- The doctrine came into effect in 1968 when *Warsaw Pact* forces crushed the Czech democratic reform movement. It was also used to justify intervention in *Afghanistan* (1979).

TIP The Brezhnev Doctrine revealed a flaw in the Soviet claim that Eastern European communism was totally unified because, in practice, the USSR was prepared to stop any country in the Warsaw Pact seeking independence from Moscow. This, in turn, suggested that countries behind the *Iron Curtain* remained communist only because they were forced to.

brinkmanship: a 1950s US policy of not backing down during a crisis, even if it meant taking the nation to the brink of war.
- *Eisenhower*, along with Secretary of State John Foster *Dulles*, took a belligerent approach to diplomacy and emphasised the need for airpower and nuclear weaponry.
- The most famous (and dangerous) example of brinkmanship was President *Kennedy's* stance during the *Cuban Missile Crisis* (1962).

DS **Britain, Battle of, 1940:** a decisive air battle over southern England.
- Hitler had to win control of the skies above the English Channel before a sea-borne German invasion could take place.
- British victory resulted in the permanent postponement of Operation Sealion, the German invasion plan.

DS **British Expeditionary Force (BEF):** a 100,000 strong professional army that was rushed to Belgium immediately after the outbreak of the *Great War* (1914–18).
- The BEF's main task was to defend the town of *Mons*, which lay directly in the path of the German advance.
- Stubborn resistance against heavy odds and a slow fighting retreat held up the Germans. However, by Christmas 1914 much of the original force had been killed or wounded.

TIP Kaiser *William II* referred to the BEF as a 'contemptible little army', yet the German General von Kluck said it was the BEF — more than anything else — that had prevented him from capturing Paris.

DS **brownshirt:** the uniform of the SA, or *Sturmabteilung* (storm troopers), the paramilitary wing of the Nazi Party.

- The SA was formed in 1921 and led by Ernst Roehm until he was killed during the *Night of the Long Knives* (1934).
- The SA attacked and disrupted the political meetings of *Hitler's* enemies — namely the German communists — and marched through the streets gathering recruits and intimidating political opponents.
- After 1934 the brownshirts were absorbed into the *SS*.

TIP The SA played a key role in the rise of *National Socialism* during the 1920s and 1930s.

DS **Brüning, Heinrich:** German chancellor (1930–32).

- Brüning was a social, political and economic conservative appointed by President *Hindenburg* to tackle Germany's economic problems.
- His approach was to cut social services and unemployment benefits. This led to his nickname as the Hunger Chancellor.
- In search of a secure political majority, Brüning dismissed the *Reichstag*, or German parliament, in July 1930. His failure to curb economic depression led to his removal in May 1932.

TIP Brüning's policies played a part in driving the hungry and jobless into the ranks of the extremists.

Brusilov Offensive, 1916: a Russian attack against the Austrians that brought temporary Russian gains and heavy Austrian losses.

- The military campaign lasted almost 3 months and saw the Russians drive deep into Austria. Romania was impressed by the success of the offensive and joined the Allied cause.
- Russia's inferior railway system prevented the Russians from reinforcing their gains quickly enough to stop decisive German intervention in support of Austria.

TIP The offensive was a turning point in Russia's war fortunes and marked the end of support for the war among the Russian people. Massive casualties convinced many Russians that their government cared little for their welfare.

buffer state: a state that sits in between two rival powers.

- In 1939 Poland was a buffer state between Germany and the *Soviet Union*.

Cambodia: a Southeast Asian republic formerly known as Kampuchea, or the Khmer Republic.

- Cambodia gained its independence from France in 1954 and entered a long period of continuous warfare involving internal conflict and external attack.
- The Khmer Rouge, a communist group backed by China and Vietnam, overthrew a US-backed government in 1975. It then cut all ties with the outside world and murdered over a million of its own citizens.
- War with Vietnam followed in 1977, and it was not until 1991 that peace was secured and a constitutional monarchy established.

DS **Camp David Agreement, 1978:** a commitment to peace made by the Egyptian leader, *Sadat*, and the Israeli prime minister, Menachem Begin.

- The agreement came after Sadat visited Israel in November 1977 to discuss peace and Begin reciprocated with a trip to Egypt a month later.
- When peace talks stalled, President *Carter* invited Begin and Sadat to Camp David in the US.
- The main framework for a peace treaty between the two countries called for Egypt to regain *Sinai* within 3 years and Israeli forces to be withdrawn, and Israel to have free passage through the Suez Canal.
- A formal peace treaty was signed in March 1979 and both sides agreed to 'recognise each other's right to live in peace within their secure and recognised boundaries'.

TIP Sadat's role was greeted in the Arab world with bitter hostility and opposition. Muslim fundamentalists assassinated him on 6 October 1981.

capitalism: an economic system based on the private ownership of property, business and industry.

- In a capitalist state the government has little role to play in the economy. This can lead to social injustice.

TIP Capitalism is practised by much of the world, and it is the ideological enemy of *communism*.

DS **Carter, James (Jimmy):** Democratic US president (1977–81).

- Carter's greatest *foreign policy* success was the *Camp David Agreement* (1978).
- He signed SALT II with *Brezhnev*, thereby limiting the number of long-range missiles each side could have in their arsenal.
- The Soviet invasion of *Afghanistan* in 1979 led to US protests and the US *Congress* refusing to ratify SALT II.
- Carter's greatest failure was the US Embassy hostage crisis of 1979–81. This followed the Iranian revolution in 1979 when Islamic radicals, under the leadership of Ayatollah Khomeini, overthrew the US-backed government.

Casablanca Conference, 1943: a meeting between *Churchill* and *Roosevelt*, 14–24 January 1943 in North Africa.

- Churchill and Roosevelt agreed that Italy should be invaded rather than northern France and that they would insist on an unconditional surrender by Germany.

TIP Unconditional surrender prevented the Germans from complaining that the post-1945 peace settlement was a *diktat*, as they had done in 1918.

Castro, Fidel: a communist revolutionary who established a Cuban socialist state in 1959 and has ruled there ever since.

- Castro led the 26 July Movement that overthrew Batista, the US-backed dictator, and confiscated US-owned land and oil companies.
- Castro's unpopularity with the US led to numerous CIA-backed attempts to assassinate him.
- His friendship with *Khrushchev* encouraged the Soviets to send nuclear missiles and military personnel to Cuba. This resulted in the *Cuban Missile Crisis* (1962).
- Castro has repeatedly sought to export his brand of *socialism* around the world, including Latin America and southern Africa.

TIP Castro is a throwback to the *Cold War* (1945–91). He is one of the last remaining revolutionaries and leads one of the world's few remaining communist states.

DS **CCC:** see *Civilian Conservation Corps.*

cede: when one state is forced to give up possession of land to another.

- Czechoslovakia was forced to cede the *Sudetenland* to Germany in 1938.

CENTO: see *Central Treaty Organisation.*

Central Intelligence Agency (CIA): a US intelligence-gathering body set up in 1947 to fight the *Cold War* (1945–91) using espionage and other behind-the-scenes operations.

Central Powers: an alliance of Germany, Austria–Hungary, Bulgaria and the Turkish Empire that fought the Allies during the *Great War* (1914–18).

Central Treaty Organisation (CENTO): known first as the Baghdad Pact (1958), this was an economic and military alliance between the US, Britain, Pakistan, Turkey, Iran and Iraq.

- Owing to Pakistan, Turkey, Iran and Iraq's close proximity to the *Soviet Union*, CENTO was a key ingredient of *containment.*

TIP

Longstanding hostility between some of the member states meant CENTO remained a loosely bound alliance. It effectively dissolved when Iran, Pakistan and Turkey withdrew in 1979.

Chamberlain, Neville: Conservative prime minister of Britain (1937–40).

- Chamberlain is closely associated with the policy of *appeasement*.
- Chamberlain served as chancellor of the exchequer in the *National Government* (1931–37) and met *Hitler* on three separate occasions in an attempt to defuse rising international tension. In 1938 Chamberlain signed the *Munich Agreement*. The British people treated him like a hero on his return. In his words, the agreement guaranteed 'peace in our time'.
- Britain, struggling to recover from the *Depression*, was militarily and emotionally unprepared for war, particularly on behalf of a faraway country. Twenty years after the *Great War* (1914–18), there was little popular support for another conflict with Germany.
- Appeasement ended in March 1939, following the German invasion of Czechoslovakia. It can be argued that it was not a failure, as it bought Britain much-needed time. Chamberlain's greatest single failure was his inability to secure an alliance with the *Soviet Union* before 1939. This would, in effect, have surrounded Germany.

TIP

Debate on the causes of the *Second World War* (1939–45) should not focus solely on appeasement. Historians have traditionally been harsh on Chamberlain and the argument that he had little option but to do what he did should be considered.

Chanak Crisis, 1922: an Anglo-Turkish conflict that brought the two countries to the brink of war.

- The Treaty of *Sevres* (1920) gave the port of Smyrna and other Turkish territory to the Greeks. Turkish nationalists led by *Kemal* were determined to overthrow both the treaty and the ruling sultan of Turkey.
- To protect their interests in the region, the British and Greek governments backed the sultan.
- Kemal's seizure of power and subsequent victory over the Greeks at Smyrna left only Britain to stop Turkey from invading southeastern Europe.
- The Dominions' (Australia, Canada, New Zealand and South Africa) refusal to join a military campaign against the Turks left British forces outnumbered and surrounded at the port of Chanak. Both sides eventually agreed to a truce and the crisis ended.

TIP

The fact that Kemal was able successfully to challenge the peace treaties — Sevres was replaced by the Treaty of *Lausanne* (1923) — was noticed around Europe and particularly in the other defeated countries.

C

DS **Cheka:** the secret police force set up by *Lenin* in 1918 to strengthen Bolshevik control and to crush opposition to the communists.

- Cheka shot thousands of people in what became known as the Red Terror; priests, landowners and supporters of the tsar were especially targeted.
- Its most famous victims were Tsar *Nicholas II* and his family, who were executed in 1918.
- Between 1922 and 1954, Cheka had several name and leadership changes before ending up as the *KGB*.

DS **Chiang Kai Shek:** a Chinese *Guomindang* leader (1927–49) who lost power to Mao *Zedong* following a civil war.

- Chiang led a corrupt and inefficient government that introduced few reforms to a country that desperately needed change.
- The 1920s and 1930s witnessed a violent struggle for power between the nationalists and communists. The two sides temporarily united from 1937 to 1945 to fight the common enemy, Japan.
- The civil war resumed in 1945 and — despite millions of dollars of US military aid to Chiang — it ended in a communist victory in 1949.
- Chiang was forced to flee to the island of Formosa (Taiwan) where he founded Nationalist China.

TIP

Guomindang's fall came at the height of the *Cold War* (1945–91). Fear that China might be followed by communist victories in Southeast Asia, the Middle East, South America and Africa convinced the *Truman* administration that *containment* had to become a global policy.

DS **Churchill, Winston:** the Conservative prime minister of Britain (1940–45 and 1951–55) who led his country to victory in the *Second World War*.

- Churchill was first sea lord (1911–15) until forced to resign following the Gallipoli campaign.
- Churchill became prime minister of a *coalition government* in May 1940, after *Chamberlain's* resignation.
- Churchill's leadership and uncompromising hostility towards *Hitler* summed up the British people's attitude during the war.
- Churchill was a harsh critic of *communism* and made the phrase *Iron Curtain* famous.
- *Stalin, Roosevelt* (and then *Truman*), and Churchill attended the *Tehran* (1943), *Yalta* and *Potsdam* conferences (1945).

TIP

Churchill was an early, persistent and vocal critic of *appeasement*. However, his controversial political career before 1937 made him an unlikely choice to succeed Chamberlain.

CIA: see *Central Intelligence Agency*.

DS **Civilian Conservation Corps, 1933:** set up as the first of the 'alphabet agencies' to provide relief to the unemployed in the US.

- Over 2.5 million men were put to work planting trees, clearing camping grounds and beaches, and building reservoirs and dams.
- Workers were given $1 per day pocket money and were required to send $25 home each month to their parents.

TIP Along with relief payments to needy citizens and public works programs, the CCC was an important component of the *First Hundred Days* that set the pace for *Roosevelt's* response to the *Depression*.

DS **Civil Rights Acts:** a series of laws passed by *Congress* to bring greater equity and justice to black Americans and other minority groups.

- The first such acts had been passed in 1866 and 1875 and established African–American citizenship and the right to vote.
- More acts were passed in 1957 and 1960 during the *Eisenhower* administration.
- In 1964, President *Johnson* signed a Civil Rights Act that outlawed discrimination in public accommodations and in employment on the basis of colour, religion, sex, race or national origin.

TIP The pursuit of civil rights in the US has tested the often difficult relationship between federal and state governments.

DS **Civil Works Administration (CWA), 1933:** a part of the *New Deal* set up to supervise government-organised job schemes.

- Work was provided for 4 million US citizens on public works schemes, such as the building of roads, schools and other publicly-owned utilities.
- The CWA was not universally popular; opponents claimed that the cost of work relief was greater than the cost of giving the unemployed dole money.

TIP Because the CWA was a temporary measure — it was replaced by the *Works Progress Administration* in 1935 — 4 million people again found themselves out of work when it was disbanded.

Clemenceau, Georges: the French prime minister (1906–09 and 1917–20) who led his country to victory in the *Great War* (1914–18).

- Clemenceau's aggressive nature earned him the nickname Le Tigre, or Tiger.
- His hatred towards Germany strongly affected his position during negotiations for the Treaty of *Versailles* (1919). He demanded harsh punishments and this brought him into conflict with Woodrow *Wilson*, who wanted a more balanced and just peace.

TIP The German people neither forgot nor forgave the Treaty of Versailles and they responded enthusiastically to *Hitler's* promise to 'tear it up'.

coalition government: a government made up of two or more political parties in order to govern because no single party has a majority.

- The *National Government* (1931–37) in Britain is a good example of a coalition.

TIP Coalition governments typically find it difficult to reach consensus on any given issue and do not usually last in office for very long.

Cold War: the state of mutual mistrust that existed from 1945 to 1991 between the US and the *Soviet Union*.

- The Cold War first developed in Germany following the *Berlin Airlift* (1948–49).
- Both sides stopped short of direct military confrontation and instead tried to undermine each other through local wars such as the *Vietnam War* (1946–75) and the *Korean War* (1950–53).
- Billions of dollars and roubles were spent on propaganda, subversion, espionage, threats and the *arms race*, before the collapse of *communism* ended the conflict in 1991.

TIP The latter half of the twentieth century was dominated by the Cold War. Virtually every international conflict during that time can be linked to it.

collaborate: to work closely with another individual or group.

- During the *Second World War* (1939–45), anti-Semites and those who supported Nazi policies were often active collaborators in German-occupied countries.

collective security: the idea that in order to safeguard world peace, all countries would agree to go to the defence of another if it was subjected to international aggression.

TIP Collective security was an integral part of the Covenant (aims, rules and procedures) of the *League of Nations* (1920–45). The unwillingness of member states to follow through was a major factor in the failure of the league as a peacekeeping organisation.

DS **collectivisation:** the policy of establishing the ownership of means of agricultural production for the state.

- Collectivisation was part of *Stalin's* attempt to modernise the *Soviet* economy after 1928.
- At the heart of collectivisation was the *kolkhoz*, or collective farm, formed when peasants pooled their private land, machinery and livestock to be placed under the ownership of the workers. The larger-scale collective farm, called a *sovkhoz*, was owned directly by the state. By 1937 most farms had been collectivised.
- The policy was bitterly opposed by the richer peasants, or *kulak* class, which destroyed livestock and produce rather than hand it over to the state.
- Stalin responded harshly. By 1934 some 5 million *kulaks* had starved to death and another 3 million were imprisoned in labour camps.

TIP Collectivisation brought mixed results for the Soviet economy and led to strong criticism of Stalin.

colonialism: the policy of obtaining territory (colonies) beyond the frontiers of a country and maintaining political, economic and military control over it.

DS **Comecon:** the Council for Mutual Economic Assistance (1949–89), set up by *Stalin* to link the economies of European communist states to that of the *Soviet Union*.

- Comecon was Stalin's response to *Marshall Aid*.
- Each *satellite* state was required to focus its agricultural and industrial production according to Stalin's demands.

TIP Stalin wanted to use it as the basis for a common economic policy, but opposition from Bulgaria and Romania — which felt the proposal undermined the sovereignty of member states — prevented this.

DS **Cominform:** the Communist Information Bureau (1947–56), which coordinated activities between the communist parties of Eastern Europe.

- In 1948 Yugoslavia was expelled because *Tito* refused to toe the line and instead followed policies different from those of the *Soviet Union*.
- Cominform was disbanded following *Stalin's* death in an attempt to reconcile the *satellite* governments with Moscow.

TIP Stalin set up Cominform because he was concerned that the *Truman Doctrine* would weaken his control over the satellite countries.

DS **Comintern:** the Communist International (1919–43), an organisation set up by *Lenin* to spread communist ideas and revolution around the world.

- Comintern's most notable act came in 1934 when it called for a 'popular front against fascism' because Stalin wanted communist parties abroad to assist left-wing and socialist organisations to fight *National Socialism* and *fascism*.
- The organisation failed to spread communism beyond the borders of the *Soviet Union*.

TIP Stalin disbanded the Comintern during the *Second World War* (1939–45) in order to improve relations with his allies.

communism: a political philosophy that rose to prominence and then collapsed during the span of the twentieth century.

- Communism adheres to the notion of a classless society based on public ownership of most property, business and industry. See also *Marx*.

concentration camps: heavily guarded prisons to hold political opponents.

- The British introduced concentration camps in the Boer War (1899–1902).
- Concentration camps were a fundamental part of the Nazi terror state.
- The first Nazi concentration camp was at Dachau. It and others housed communists, Jews, homosexuals and other so-called enemies of the Nazis.

TIP There was an important functional difference between the two types of camps operated by the Nazis. While killings of inmates certainly took place at concentration camps, it was in the *death camps* such as *Auschwitz–Birkenau* that millions of human beings were systematically exterminated. See also *Holocaust*.

DS **Congress:** a meeting of delegates to the national parliament of the United States that is divided into the Senate and the House of Representatives.

- Each of the 50 US states elects two senators to the senate for a 6-year term. Members to the House of Representatives are elected every 2 years.
- The number of seats each state is allocated in the House of Representatives is determined by population density. A total of 435 seats are available.
- The House of Representatives concerns itself primarily with financial matters while the Senate oversees *foreign policy*.

TIP Congress is the legislative (law-making) branch of the US government; the other two branches are the judiciary (legal system) and the executive (presidency).

conscription: sometimes known as national service, it is compulsory enlistment for military service.

- The idea of conscription dates back to the era of the French Revolution when the Committee for Public Safety issued a decree providing for mobilisation of all Frenchmen.
- Compulsory enlistment allows a government to call on large numbers of trained civilians in anticipation of imminent war.
- In the First World War, Britain was the last European power to introduce conscription (1916), in response to dwindling numbers of volunteers and high casualties.

TIP Conscription remained one of the last bastions of government power over the citizen and went against the trend of increased liberalism during the later nineteenth century.

DS **Conservative Party:** a British political organisation dating back to the 1830s.

- After 1886, the Conservative Party was generally known as Conservative and Unionist because of its opposition to Irish Home Rule.
- The party supports a free-enterprise economy, property ownership and strong military defence. Historically, the Conservatives have concentrated on foreign and imperial affairs.
- *Thatcher's* leadership in the 1980s saw the Conservative Party move more to the right and away from its traditional support of existing institutions and moderate reforms.

TIP Knowledge of the Conservative Party is important to understanding the course of twentieth-century British history.

constitution: a written statement of principles that govern a state.

- The primary purpose of a constitution is to set the limits of state power and safeguard the rights of the state's subjects.

containment: the backbone of US *foreign policy* to stop the spread of *communism* to other regions of the world.

- Containment was the cornerstone of President *Truman's* foreign policy. He supplied money, weapons and advisers to friendly states to help them hem in the *Soviet Union* and its allies.
- See also *Truman Doctrine*.

TIP The introduction of containment in 1947 marked the permanent end of the USA's traditional isolationism and demonstrated its preparedness to play a leading role in international relations.

DS **Coolidge, Calvin:** the US Republican vice-president (1921–23) who became president (1923–29) following *Harding's* mid-term death.

- Coolidge oversaw the *boom* years in the US by supporting unrestricted freedom in business; this led to mass production of a range of consumer goods. His *foreign policy* was one of *isolationism*.
- His policies did not survive the *Wall Street Crash* (1929).

TIP Not everyone did well under Coolidge; millions of US citizens continued to live in poverty between 1923 and 1929.

corporate state: an attempt by *Mussolini* to resolve social and economic conflict in Italy during the 1920s.

- Twenty-two corporations were created (primarily in industry and agriculture) in which both owners and workers were represented.

TIP Mussolini created the corporate state to take away the rights of workers to join trade unions, thereby undermining opposition to his consolidation of power.

Council of Europe: an organisation of West European states set up in 1949 to increase unity between members.

- The council meets to discuss a range of matters of common interest, such as education and public health issues.
- Its single most important achievement has been the establishment of the European Convention for the Protection of Human Rights (1950).

TIP Do not see the council as a move towards European integration; it had no authority over member states and was simply a further step in European cooperation.

***coup d'état*:** 'blow against the state' in translation, the term refers to a sudden, violent and/or illegal change of leadership by an individual or a group.

- The *Beer Hall Putsch* (1923) is an example of an attempted coup.

Croatia: a region of the former Yugoslavia in the northern Balkans.

- Before the *Great War* (1914–18), the Austrians ruled Croatia; it became part of the Yugoslav state after 1919.
- During the *Second World War* (1939–45), Croatian nationalists collaborated with the occupying Germans in the hope of breaking free from Yugoslavia. This led to atrocities against Serbs, Jews and communists.

- In 1946, Croatia declared itself a people's republic within communist Yugoslavia, where it remained until the death of *Tito*. Croatia declared its independence in 1991, a decision that led to war with Serbia.

Cuban Missile Crisis, 1962: a stand-off between the *Soviet Union* and the US that brought the world to the brink of *nuclear war*.

- The crisis was sparked by *Castro's* decision to allow *Khrushchev* to place nuclear missiles on Cuba, a move that put the USA's major east-coast cities in range of attack.
- *Kennedy* considered a range of responses, from doing nothing to full-scale invasion of Cuba and the risk of starting a third world war. He chose an air and sea blockade of Cuba.
- Following a 13-day confrontation, Khrushchev was the first to back down when Soviet missiles were removed from Cuba in return for the removal of US missiles in Turkey.
- The crisis demonstrated the dangers of *brinkmanship*. The *Nuclear Test Ban Treaty* (1963) followed, along with a direct telephone hotline between the White House and the Kremlin.

TIP

The fact that Kennedy was prepared to stand up to Khrushchev led to greater cooperation between the two men and a slight, albeit temporary, thaw in the *Cold War* (1945–91).

DS **Cultural Revolution, 1966–69:** a period of social, political and economic upheaval in China initiated by Mao *Zedong*.

- Mao wanted to purge the Chinese Communist Party of suspected conservatives who opposed his policies and to educate young Chinese about his theories. The People's Liberation Army (PLA) helped form Red Guard units of students who sought out those they suspected of not being true communists.
- To guide them, each guard was given a copy of the *Little Red Book*, which contained the quotations of Chairman Mao.
- The Cultural Revolution soon went out of control. Temples and churches were burned down and hundreds of show trials took place. In some towns fighting broke out between workers and Red Guards and it was not until 1969 that the Cultural Revolution finally ran its course and ended.

TIP

Mao was able to strengthen his hold on power, but only at major cost to Chinese industrial production and government education programmes.

DS **CWA:** see *Civil Works Administration*.

D'Annunzio, Gabriele: an Italian war hero who led a group of ex-soldiers to seize the port of *Fiume* in September 1919.

- Although forced by the Italian government to leave 2 years later, the regime he set up in Fiume was a model for Italian fascists.

TIP

> Widespread popular support for D'Annunzio's actions further undermined public confidence in an Italian government already weakened by corruption and economic problems.

Danzig: a port city and the site of a dispute that contributed to the outbreak of the *Second World War* (1939–45).

- The city was part of Germany but — in order to allow the Poles access to the Baltic Sea — it was made a 'free city' by the Treaty of *Versailles* (1919).
- The Polish Corridor separated Germany from Danzig and its largely German-speaking population. *Hitler* demanded possession of the corridor and Danzig, but the Poles refused.
- Hitler used Poland's defiance — as well as false stories of Polish abuses of Danzig's German citizens — as the pretext for a full invasion of Poland on 1 September 1939.

> Hitler's fear that the *Soviet Union* might support Poland in a war against Germany led him to forge the *Nazi–Soviet Pact* (1939).

Dardanelles: see ANZAC.

Dawes Plan: a set of recommendations that followed an international conference led by American economist Charles Dawes to discuss Germany's post-1918 economic problems.

- In 1923 the German economy was in ruins. In order for Germany to pay realistic war *reparations*, the plan recommended a reduction in the original figure to a more manageable rate. It also proposed a reorganisation of the German currency and international loans to Germany to help kick-start its economy.
- The *Young Plan* (1929) further reduced German war reparations.

TIP The plan only gave Germany superficial and temporary relief from its debt problem. The US money that poured into Germany simply went around in circles — the Germans used it to pay reparations to the French and British who, in turn, used it to repay war loans to the USA.

D-Day, 6 June 1944: the Allied landings in Normandy during the *Second World War* (1939–45).

- The invasion of German-occupied France opened a second front in the war and forced *Hitler* to divert troops and equipment from the Eastern Front.
- The Allies drove steadily east through France and Belgium and within a year Germany surrendered, but only after much heavy fighting and losses on both sides.

death camps: facilities built throughout eastern and central Europe by the Nazis during the *Second World War* (1939–45) to expedite the implementation of the *Final Solution*. See also *Auschwitz–Birkenau* and *genocide*.

decolonisation: the process by which the peoples of European-governed colonies gained the right to self-rule and independence.

- Wide-scale decolonisation began at the end of the *Second World War* (1939–45).

TIP The *Cold War* (1945–91) and decolonisation were the two issues that dominated international relations between 1945 and 1990.

DS **Defence of the Realm Act (DORA), 1914:** a series of measures introduced by the *Asquith* government to give the state increased control over its citizens during the *Great War* (1914–18).

- DORA allowed the authorities to take over the country's coalmines and railways, to censor information and to control wages and prices.
- In order to limit drunkenness (which affected war production), the legislation cut pub opening hours and ordered beer to be watered down to make it less alcoholic.

demilitarised zone: an area that must remain free of troops, weapons or fortifications.

- The Treaty of *Versailles* (1919) demilitarised the *Rhineland*. It was remilitarised by *Hitler* in 1936.

TIP The absence of French and British opposition to German troops in the Rhineland was a feature of *appeasement* that greatly boosted Hitler's confidence.

democracy: a political philosophy that government should be chosen by the people through free elections with the participation of an unlimited number of political parties.

DS **Democratic Party:** one of the two main US political parties with roots going back to the 1820s.

- The Democrats emerged from the *Wall Street Crash* (1929) as the party prepared to take action to end unemployment and stimulate industry. This action was

embodied in the *New Deal*, which helped propel the Democrats to continuous spells in office from 1933 to 1953.

- Under Democratic presidents *Wilson*, *Roosevelt*, *Truman* and *Kennedy*, the US steadily retreated from its traditional isolationist *foreign policy*.
- The most recent Democratic president was Bill Clinton (1993–2000).

DS **Deng Xiao Peng:** the leader of communist China (1976–98) following the death of Mao *Zedong*.

- Deng came to office following a power struggle with the Gang of Four — a group led by Mao's widow — who wanted a revival of the *Cultural Revolution*.
- More interested in economic growth than in fostering a revolutionary spirit, Deng encouraged foreign countries to invest in China.
- While economic conditions improved under Deng, the political situation in China changed little. In April 1989, a demonstration in *Tiananmen Square* in Beijing called for increased political freedom. When Deng sent soldiers to break up the demonstration, between 500 and 1,000 civilians were killed.

TIP An understanding of Deng's leadership is essential to explaining why China has increasingly opened up to the West.

Depression: the sudden collapse of international trade and the rapid increase in unemployment that affected millions worldwide throughout the 1930s.

- The *Wall Street Crash* (1929) led to an unprecedented global economic slump.
- Still suffering the economic legacy of the *Great War* (1914–18), Europeans were especially badly affected. Millions lost their jobs and successive governments seemed incapable of leading recovery.
- Conditions began to ease in the late 1930s when more and more people returned to work as governments increased defence spending in response to the rising threat of war.

TIP The Depression's souring effects on international relations continued for almost a decade. It is important to remember how economic factors led increasingly to peace being threatened, and ultimately contributed to the outbreak of the *Second World War* (1939–45).

DS **desegregation:** also known as *integration*, this policy aimed to end the separation of US society along racial, religious or political lines.

- In 1948, President *Truman* officially banned segregation in the US military. Other than this, however, little government action was taken to raise black Americans from their long-time position as second-class citizens.
- In 1954, the *Supreme Court* ordered the end of segregation in education.
- Two years later, the same court announced that segregation on buses was illegal. This decision followed the widely publicised boycott of buses in Alabama. Two key figures were Rosa Parks and Martin Luther *King*.
- In 1957, President *Eisenhower* sent troops to Little Rock in Arkansas to enforce desegregation in the school system.

TIP Desegregation is a cornerstone of the history of the struggle for civil rights in the USA.

DS **destalinisation:** an attack by *Khrushchev* against the policies introduced by his predecessor, Stalin.

- The policy was announced in Khruschev's speech to the twentieth Congress of the Soviet Communist Party in 1956. He aimed to bring about greater individual freedom by discrediting his predecessor.
- Khrushchev reduced the power of the secret police and ordered the dismantling of many state-run labour camps.
- A sure sign that the *Soviet Union* was being destalinised was the fact that Khrushchev's political opponents were not executed.

TIP Destalinisation should not be mistaken as a move towards greater democratisation of the Soviet Union. Moves toward liberalisation in the *satellite* states of Poland and Hungary were crushed when they used Khrushchev's policies to push for greater independence from Moscow.

détente: the easing of tension between the *Soviet Union* and United States from 1964 to the mid-1970s.

- The *Cuban Missile Crisis* (1962) demonstrated the danger of military confrontation in the nuclear age.
- Other factors contributed to a thaw in relations. Both *superpowers* had economic problems during the 1970s, with the US enduring increased inflation and the Soviet Union spending 20% of its national budget on defence. Moreover, the US was looking to end its role in the *Vietnam War* (1946–75) while the USSR had begun to fall out with neighbouring China.
- These factors, along with a series of arms-reduction negotiations during the 1970s, led to a somewhat more relaxed international atmosphere.
- *Détente* ended abruptly in 1979 with the Soviet invasion of *Afghanistan,* and there was a renewal of *Cold War* hostility.

deterrence: the US policy of curbing hostile *Soviet* behaviour during the *Cold War* (1945–91) by the possession of a large arsenal of nuclear weapons.

- After the *Soviet Union* detonated its first *atomic bomb* in 1949, both sides were deterred from attacking the other by the prospect of *mutually assured destruction* (MAD).

Diem, Ngo Dinh: South Vietnam leader (1956–63).

- Diem led a corrupt and inefficient government that favoured Catholics in an overwhelmingly Buddhist country.
- He was initially considered an important US ally in the fight against communism. However, his increasingly blatant corruption and refusal to introduce social and political reform to South Vietnam alienated Diem from the US, which was already dissatisfied with his inability to tackle the communist threat.
- Diem was overthrown in 1963 and executed in a CIA-backed plot.

TIP Diem's failure to defeat communism led *Kennedy* and *Johnson* to escalate US military involvement in the region.

Dien Bien Phu: a Vietnamese town that was the scene of a decisive battle between French forces and the *Vietminh* in 1954.

- After years of *guerrilla warfare* against the Vietnamese communists, the French were militarily defeated at Dien Bien Phu. This loss convinced the French government that the time had come to withdraw from Southeast Asia.

TIP Between 1950 and 1954, the US provided the French with $1.2 billion of military aid. The French defeat marked a turning point in US involvement in Vietnam and pushed it from financial backing to direct military participation.

dictator: a political leader who has sole and total power and who does not tolerate dissent or opposition to his or her form of government.

- Examples of twentieth-century dictators include *Stalin, Hitler, Mussolini* and *Chiang*.

diktat: a 'categorical order' that refers to a victor imposing harsh peace terms on the vanquished.

- Diktat specifically relates to the widespread German sentiment that the Treaty of *Versailles* (1919) had left the country humiliated and defenceless.

TIP German anger at the victors' denial of their negotiation rights at Versailles was deep, and contributed significantly to *Hitler's* political appeal.

disarmament: the reduction of weapons of war carried out by one or more states to promote international peace and security.

- The interwar period witnessed several attempts at disarmament involving the democracies and the dictatorships.
- The proliferation of nuclear weapons during the *Cold War* (1945–91) led to several agreements between the *Soviet Union* and the US, most notably the *Nuclear Test Ban Treaty* (1963), SALT I (1972) and II (1979) and the INF Treaty (1987).

TIP Attempts at disarmament met with only limited success as countries frequently squabbled over whether disarmament should be unilateral (one side only) or multilateral (i.e., no one country should begin to disarm until all countries agree to do so).

Dolfuss, Engelbert: a right-wing Austrian chancellor who was murdered by Austrian Nazis in 1934 during an attempted coup.

- Austrian Nazis hoped *Hitler* would actively intervene in support of their seizure of power. Dolfuss had close ties with *Mussolini*, who at that time distrusted Hitler and was not yet his ally. Mussolini warned Hitler he would go to war with Germany over Austria and forced him to back down.
- Dolfuss's murder and the attempted coup increased British and French concern

about Hitler's ambitions. The two countries formed the *Stresa Front* (1935) with Mussolini and pledged themselves to defend Austrian *sovereignty*.

TIP Hitler remained determined to carry out the *Anschluss* (1938) but realised he could only do so with Mussolini at his side and he began his courtship of the fascist leader.

domino theory: the *Cold War* (1945–91) notion that the fall of one country to *communism* would lead automatically to the collapse of other countries in the same region.

- *Eisenhower* first used the term in 1954 to justify US involvement in Southeast Asia, particularly Vietnam.
- Under *Kennedy* and *Johnson*, the domino theory underpinned US *foreign policy*. It received increased credence in 1973, in response to sustained communist presence in Laos and South Vietnam.

TIP Use the theory to explain US foreign policy during the 1960s.

DS **DORA:** see *Defence of the Realm Act*.

DS **dreadnought:** a class of battleship launched by Britain in 1906.

- The first new ship, HMS *Dreadnought*, was quicker, better armed and had thicker protective armour than any previous warship.

TIP Britain's main rival at the time, Germany, was determined to compete on near terms and set about developing new ships of its own. This led to a naval *arms race* that was a major cause of the *Great War* (1914–18).

Dubcek, Alexander: a communist leader of Czechoslovakia whose ideas for improving his country's economy led to the Prague Spring (1968).

- As first secretary of the Communist Party, Dubcek's proposed reforms included: more decentralised economic planning, greater individual freedoms, increased contacts with the West, and modernising the Czech Communist Party. He called these reforms 'Socialism with a human face' and assured Soviet leaders that Czechoslovakia was committed to the *Warsaw Pact*.
- The term Prague Spring described the feeling that Czechoslovakia was being reborn.
- Despite Dubcek's assurances, the Soviet leadership was concerned about the Prague Spring's possible knock-on effects in other communist countries. The USSR was not prepared to wait and see and its forces invaded Czechoslovakia in August 1968. Dubcek was forced out and replaced with Gustav Husak, a hard-liner who abolished the reforms.

TIP The Soviet invasion of Czechoslovakia brought an end to *détente* and marked a deterioration in relations between Moscow and Washington.

DS **Dulles, John Foster:** the US secretary of state (1953–59) who was guided by the belief that *communism* needed to be actively countered wherever it appeared.

- Dulles saw US *foreign policy* resting on three fundamental tenets: first, *containment*; second, 'roll back', which offered active help and support to the peoples of Eastern Europe if they rose up against Soviet control; and 'massive retaliation', which took the lessons of the *Korean War* (1950–53) to suggest that the US was prepared to respond to a Soviet threat with nuclear force.

TIP Dulles's policies safeguarded both West Berlin and the government of the nationalist Chinese against communist threats.

DS **Duma:** a Russian parliament called for by *Nicholas II* in his *October Manifesto* (1905) following the *Revolution of 1905.*

- The Duma convened a total of four times between 1906 and 1914. When the first Duma reminded Nicholas II of his promise to introduce constitutional government, he dismissed it. The second Duma (1907) was treated similarly when the revolutionaries won 65 seats.
- Changes to electoral reform by the pro-tsarist prime minister, *Stolypin,* ensured the third and fourth Dumas supported Nicholas II.
- The *Provisional Government* (1917) was formed by the Duma in March 1917.
- The Duma was reinstated as the foundation of Russian government following the fall of *communism* in 1991.

TIP A good explanation for the overthrow of Tsar Nicholas II must include knowledge of the Duma's role.

Dunkirk: the northern French port from which over 320,000 British and French troops were evacuated between 27 May and 4 June 1940, when they were cut off and surrounded by advancing German forces.

- Some 850 vessels carried out the evacuation, over half of them privately owned and crewed and sent from England.
- While heavy equipment was abandoned, the evacuation of fighting men allowed Britain to fight on.

TIP The phrase 'Dunkirk Spirit' was used throughout the first years of the war to rally the British people to persevere in the face of seemingly overwhelming odds.

DS **Easter Uprising:** an Irish republican rebellion in Dublin in 1916.

- The aim of the rebels was to secure immediate independence from Britain. They hoped — falsely — that Germany would come to their aid.
- Several days (24–29 April) of heavy fighting took place around the General Post Office before British troops restored order.
- Fourteen leaders of the rebellion were executed and many others imprisoned.

TIP The Easter Uprising is one of the most celebrated events in the Republican calendar and a key feature of the conflict in Ireland.

DS **Ebert, Friedrich:** the first president (1919–25) of the *Weimar Republic* (1918–33).

- Ebert survived the turbulence of the immediate postwar period in Germany, including numerous attempts to overthrow the government, hyperinflation and French occupation of the *Ruhr* (1923).

TIP Ebert unleashed the *Freikorps* to help defeat the *Spartacist Uprising* in 1919.

EEC: see *European Economic Community*.

DS **Eichmann, Adolf:** an *SS* officer who, as head of the *Gestapo's* Jewish Evacuation Department, planned and oversaw the arrest, transportation and execution of Jews.

- Eichmann was a key figure at the *Wannsee Conference* (1942).
- He chose personally to supervise *Auschwitz–Birkenau* for several weeks in order to appreciate it at first hand.
- In 1961 Israeli agents kidnapped Eichmann from Argentina and returned him to Israel to face trial. He was condemned to death and hanged.

TIP Eichmann was a key architect of Nazi racial policy; be prepared to explain his role in response to any question about the implementation of the *Final Solution*.

DS ***Einsatzgruppen*:** the German for 'special groups of soldiers', they were the *SS* and police who followed the German army into occupied Europe in search of those they defined as enemies of the state.

- Between 1939 and 1941 they travelled throughout Poland murdering national

leaders and forcing Jews into ghettos. Following the invasion of Russia in 1941 they were ordered to exterminate all Jews and Soviet political leaders under German jurisdiction.

- The soldiers of the *Einsatzgruppen* used the term 'resettled' to describe what happened to Jews who were rounded up, transported, shot and thrown into ditches.
- The worst single atrocity took place at Babi Yar, a ravine in the Ukraine, where 30,000 Jews were shot over the course of 2 days in September 1941.

TIP The time it took to shoot large numbers of people — as well as the fact that the Germans considered this technique of massacre an unpleasant duty for the perpetrators — made the Nazis look for what they called a more 'efficient and humane' method of murder. That search led them to poison gas.

DS **Eisenhower, Dwight:** US Republican president (1953–61).

- Eisenhower rose to prominence during the *Second World War* (1939–45) as supreme commander of the Allied Expeditionary Force that landed in Normandy in 1944 and campaigned across Western Europe.
- The Russians reached Berlin, Prague and Vienna before Eisenhower's forces and he faced the criticism that his military leadership had effectively ceded bargaining power to Moscow in the postwar political settlements.
- Eisenhower was a moderate who introduced *civil rights* and social security acts. He also ended the *Korean War* (1950–53).
- In 1957 he issued the *Eisenhower Doctrine,* which stated that the US would use economic aid and military force to intervene on behalf of any Middle Eastern state threatened by *communism*. The doctrine was withdrawn 2 years later because it failed to gain Arab nationalist support.
- Eisenhower had hoped for a thaw in relations with the USSR following the death of *Stalin* in 1953. This lasted until the *Hungarian Uprising* (1956). After that, he began a build-up of US armed forces and nuclear weapons.

TIP Eisenhower launched US intervention in Vietnam and set his country on a path that ended in defeat and withdrawal in 1973.

El Alamein, Battle of, 1942: a battle that resulted in the eviction of the German military from North Africa.

- A British and New Zealand attack eventually chased the Germans out of Egypt.
- After 2 years of continuously bad war news, the victory at El Alamein was a major boost for home-front morale in Britain.

TIP This battle — with the Japanese defeat by the US at Midway Island (1942) and the Russian victory at *Stalingrad* (1943) — was one of three major military turning points in the *Second World War* (1939–45).

DS **Emergency Banking Relief Act, 1933:** the first of a vast legislative output in the USA (1933–34) that signalled the start of the *New Deal.*

- Passed by *Congress* on 9 March 1933, the act gave the government the power to regulate banking activities by inspecting the accounts of every bank in the country.
- Banks that were found to be solvent were allowed to continue in business. Those found to be in poor financial shape were either managed by the federal government or shut down.
- The Emergency Banking Relief Act was a major factor in ending the US banking crisis.

TIP See also *First Hundred Days* and *fireside chats*.

DS **Enabling Act, 1933:** a law passed by the *Hitler*-controlled *Reichstag* on 23 March 1933 that destroyed what remained of the German constitution and replaced parliamentary power with Nazi power.

- A two-thirds Reichstag majority was achieved by the exclusion of communists and the intimidating presence of the SA in the voting hall. It allowed the new government to make laws without parliamentary approval.
- Hitler used the act to get rid of anyone or anything that limited his power.

TIP The act was pivotal in moving Germany away from government by parliamentary democracy to a one-party dictatorship.

***Entente Cordiale*:** the 'friendly understanding' that defined the increasingly close relationship between Britain and France before 1914.

- At the end of the nineteenth century, relations between Britain and France were tense because of imperial competition. By 1904 they signed an agreement that ended colonial disputes and put the countries on good terms.
- *William II* tried to break up the *entente* when he challenged French control of Morocco in 1911 (see also *Agadir*). The plan backfired when Britain and France moved closer together.

TIP The *Entente Cordiale* was the first step in a series of diplomatic agreements between France and Britain that ultimately drew them into a military alliance against Germany.

Estonia: the northernmost of the three independent *Baltic States*.

- Estonia was created following the *October Revolution* (1917) and became a sovereign state in 1920.
- The *Nazi–Soviet Pact* (1939) allowed *Soviet* penetration of Estonia, and the whole country was annexed in June 1940. Two months later, Moscow announced the absorption of Estonia into the USSR, an act never recognised by the USA or Britain.
- The Germans replaced the Russians as rulers of Estonia between 1941 and 1944
- Estonian independence was achieved following the collapse of the *Soviet Union* in 1991.

Ethiopia: see *Abyssinian War* (1935–36).

European Economic Community (EEC): an organisation of Western states whose goal is greater economic cooperation among its members.

- The EEC was called for in the Treaty of Rome (1957) and set up a year later. Belgium, France, Italy, Luxemburg, the Netherlands and West Germany were the six original members.
- The key aims of the EEC charter are the abolition of tariffs in member states, free movement of capital and labour, and joint financial and social policies.
- Membership expanded in 1973 to include Britain, Ireland and Denmark; another six states had joined by 1995.

TIP The establishment of the EEC was a major step towards greater European integration and was forerunner to the European Union.

DS **Fair Labor Standards Act, 1938:** *New Deal* legislation that forbade children younger than 16 from working and established a minimum wage and 40-hour working week for many US workers.

- The act did not protect women engaged in agricultural and domestic work.

TIP This was the last important measure of the New Deal. Thereafter *Roosevelt* became increasingly concerned with foreign affairs as Europe moved closer to another war.

Falange: the Spanish Fascist Party founded by Primo de Rivero in 1933.

- The Falangist philosophy emphasised obedience to the leader, loyalty to the nation and reinforcement of national culture and identity.
- Under *Franco*, the Falange became the only legal political party in Spain.

TIP The Falange joined with the Catholic church, the army and Spain's wealthy landowners to form the *Spanish Civil War's* nationalist faction.

fascism: an extreme right-wing political movement opposed to *democracy* and liberalism.

- The characteristics of a fascist state include hatred of *communism*, one-party politics, nationalism, a strong leader, authoritarian government and militarism.
- Italy (*Mussolini*), Spain (*Franco*), Portugal (Salazar) and Germany (*Hitler*) are countries that have been ruled by fascism during the twentieth century.

DS **February Revolution, 1917:** the political and economic disorder that began in *Petrograd* (St Petersburg) to culminate in *Nicholas II's* abdication.

- In March 1917 (the old Russian calendar had the month as February), a series of strikes against low industrial wages led to over 90,000 Russians being in the streets.
- Food shortages, low pay and Russian losses in the *Great War* (1914–18) quickly turned rioting into revolution.
- The *Duma* demanded the formation of a new *Provisional Government* (1917) and the abdication of Tsar Nicholas.

TIP

The February Revolution left a political hole in Russian politics that led to bitter conflict between the various groups who aimed to fill it.

DS **Federal Emergency Relief Administration (FERA), 1933:** an organisation set up by *Congress* to help millions of unemployed US citizens.

- Joblessness was the single and most visible consequence of the *Depression*. The FERA was one of several government agencies established to tackle unemployment. Others included the CCC, the TVA, the PWA and the WPA.
- FERA provided over $500 million to the hungry and homeless; the federal government provided $1 in aid to each state for every $3 the state spent on unemployment relief.

Federal Republic of Germany (FRG): the West German state (1949–90) during the *Cold War* (1945–91).

- After defeat in the *Second World War* (1939–45), Germany was divided into four zones of occupation, each governed by one of the victorious allies (the US, Britain, France, the *Soviet Union*).
- Heightened tension led to the division of Germany into separate states.
- West Germany was modelled on the Western democracies; it received massive economic and military backing from the US and Britain and was admitted into both the EEC and NATO.
- West Germany recovered rapidly from the ravages of the war to a position of real prosperity.

TIP

Use the division of Germany to help explain the course of the Cold War in Europe.

FERA: see *Federal Emergency Relief Administration.*

DS **Final Solution:** the name given to the Nazi plan to exterminate European Jewry.

- At the end of 1941, *Einsatzgruppen* killings were felt to be slow and inefficient and the Nazi hierarchy sought a 'final solution to the Jewish question'.
- Plans drawn up at the *Wannsee Conference* (1942) called for the systematic and industrial-scale murder of European Jews and other 'undesirables'.
- Moved around by a highly developed railway network throughout the Nazi-occupied countries, victims were transported to specially built camps and killed. The slaughter was supervised and carried out by the *SS*.

TIP

The Final Solution was the final component of Hitler's goal of waging merciless war against those he felt were racially inferior to Germanic, or Aryan, people.

DS **fireside chats:** a series of radio speeches given by President *Roosevelt* directly to the US people.

- The first broadcast was on 12 March 1933 and over 60 million listeners tuned in to hear Roosevelt assure them that banks were again safe places for depositors' savings.

TIP The chats helped re-establish people's confidence in their political leadership, their banks and their economic system.

DS **First Hundred Days:** the first 3 months of the *Roosevelt* presidency that marked the beginning of the *New Deal.*

- During this time there was more government action to end the *Depression* than during the entire *Hoover* years.

TIP The First Hundred Days was vital to instilling post-Depression hope and courage among Americans.

First World War: see *Great War* (1914–18).

Fiume: a seaport on the Adriatic coast that was the centre of a political and military crisis in 1919.

- The future of this disputed city was being deliberated at the *Paris Peace Conference* (1919) when a group of Italian nationalists led by *D'Annunzio* seized and held it for nearly 2 years.
- In 1921 Fiume was made a 'free city' under the *League of Nations* (1920–45). When *Mussolini* came to power, he defied the league and incorporated the city into Italy. In 1945 it was *ceded* to Yugoslavia and is now a part of Croatia.

TIP D'Annunzio's takeover of Fiume demonstrated that the First World War victors could be defied successfully, something noted by other European nationalists.

DS **Five-Year Plans:** Stalin's organisation of the economy to modernise the *Soviet Union.*

- Three successive plans set new goals and targets for the national economy every 5 years. The overall aim was *collectivisation* of agriculture and expansion of industry, especially iron, steel and heavy industry. The first plan (1928–32) focused on these.
- The second Five-Year Plan (1933–37) aimed to provide more consumer goods for the Soviet people, while the third (1938–42) looked to strengthen military preparedness.
- A fourth plan was begun after the end of the *Second World War* (1939–45).
- The need to produce vast amounts of goods came at a cost — quantity was often achieved at the expense of quality.

TIP Successive Five-Year Plans inflicted a heavy burden on the Soviet people, who were forced to work increasingly hard for little improvement in their standard of living.

DS **Ford, Gerald:** US Republican president (1974–77).

- Ford became vice-president after Spiro Agnew, his predecessor, resigned amidst allegations of tax fraud. He entered the White House as US president when President *Nixon* resigned following the *Watergate Affair* (1974).
- During Ford's brief presidential term, he achieved little in domestic affairs.

His *foreign policy* was marked by *communism's* ascendancy in Laos, Cambodia and South Vietnam.

DS **Fordney–McCumber Tariff, 1922:** a US move to raise taxes on imports (tariffs) in order to give domestically produced goods a competitive edge over foreign goods.

- The tariff came at a time of US economic pre-eminence in the world following the *Great War* (1914–18) and targeted wheat, corn and beef imports as well as chemicals and textiles.
- It did not address the basic problem of US over-production. Instead, it led to retaliation by other countries, reinvigorated economic nationalism and, ultimately, a decline in world trade.
- The US government again raised tariffs in 1930 with the *Hawley–Smoot Tariff*. By 1932, some 25 nations had retaliated by raising tariffs in their own countries, with the result that US farmers stood little chance of selling their goods overseas. Between 1929 and 1932 there was a 40% decline in world trade.

TIP Tariffs, or duties, tend to be last-ditch economic policies as they often result in decreased international trade and increased political tension.

foreign policy: the way a government determines and guides its international relations.

- Foreign policy is typically guided by one of two approaches: isolationist — withdrawing from the international stage, and internationalist — playing a full role in global affairs.

Fourteen Points: President *Wilson's* plan for securing international peace and stability after 1918.

- The Fourteen Points were an elaboration on Wilson's two main aims: firstly, to prevent another war through open diplomacy, free trade, disarmament and free movement on the seas; secondly, to address specific problems facing post-1918 Europe, namely *national self-determination*.
- The *League of Nations* (1920–45) was a by-product of the Fourteen Points.

TIP Wilson failed to create the new world order he envisaged. The *Paris Peace Treaties* (1919) were much harsher than he had hoped for; the US Senate failed to support either the Treaty of *Versailles* (1919) or the League of Nations, choosing instead to return to a policy of *isolationism*.

Franco, Francisco: Spanish president (1939–75).

- Franco was known as *el Caudillo* (the leader) and he was commander in chief of nationalist forces during the *Spanish Civil War* (1936–39).
- Franco was supported by the clergy, the monarchists and the *Falange* in his bid to overthrow the democratically-elected republic. He also received military support from *Hitler* and *Mussolini*.
- Victory saw Franco rule as dictator until his death in 1975. He kept Spain neutral during the *Second World War* (1939–45), and in the 1960s drew his country

closer to the US by offering the US military bases in Spain in exchange for economic aid.

TIP Before his death, Franco took steps to ease Spain's transition back to monarchy and democracy.

Franz Ferdinand: the archduke and heir to the Austro-Hungarian Empire whose assassination set in motion the sequence of events that resulted in the *Great War* (1914–18).

- Franz Ferdinand and his wife were gunned down while driving through *Sarajevo* on 28 June 1914. The killer was Gavrilo Princip, a member of the Black Hand Serb terrorist group that wanted to unite the Serbian peoples of the Austro-Hungarian Empire with an independent Serbian state.
- The assassination was quickly followed by an Austro-Hungarian declaration of war against Serbia, backed by the Germans. Russia's alliance with Serbia, France and England led to war.

TIP Some students see the killing of Franz Ferdinand as the cause of the war. In reality, his assassination needs to be studied in the wider context of the *Alliance system* in order fully to understand its true significance.

DS **freedom rides:** a series of bus journeys undertaken by civil rights activists to southern stations, such as Alabama and Mississippi, in order to break laws favouring whites-only in the use of buses, public toilets, restaurants etc.

- The first ride was organised by the Congress of Racial Equality (CORE) in 1961. The riders met with violent opposition from state authorities.
- Attorney General Robert Kennedy put an end to segregation in bus and rail stations and at airports.

TIP Do not confuse CORE with the US *Congress*; the former was a non-government movement to advance civil rights for black Americans.

DS ***Freikorps*:** the private armies of German nationalist ex-soldiers raised at the end of 1918, which put a bloody end to communist attempts to overthrow the *Weimar Republic* (1918–33).

- The *Freikorps* occupied Berlin in March 1920 in support of a short-lived uprising known as the *Kapp Putsch*.
- Its members drifted into the ranks of the *brownshirts*.

TIP The ability of the *Freikorps* to function without restraint speaks volumes about the weakness of the Weimar Republic from its inception.

FRG: see *Federal Republic of Germany*.

Gallipoli: see *ANZAC.*

DS **gangsterism:** the rise of organised crime in the USA in the 1920s that was a by-product of *prohibition.*

- Criminals fought each other for control of the illegal alcohol business in cities like New York and Chicago.
- Politicians, city officials and policemen were bribed by gangsters.
- The most notorious gangster was Al Capone. His men killed seven leading members of a rival gang in the St Valentine's Day Massacre in 1929.

TIP Gangsterism was defeated primarily by the *Depression,* which left increasingly few Americans with money to spare for drinking.

DS **Gaza Strip:** an area of disputed territory on the southwest corner of Israel and the northeast border of Egypt.

- Egypt administered the Gaza Strip from 1949 to 1956. It was then occupied by Israel following the second *Arab–Israeli War.*
- The *United Nations* took control of the Gaza Strip until 1967, when Israel permanently occupied the territory after defeating the Egyptians in the *Six-Day War.*

TIP The histories of the *West Bank* and the Gaza Strip are important in explaining the Palestinian *intifada.*

GDR: German Democratic Republic, the title given to the Soviet-formed and dominated East German state (1949–90).

- Unlike its counterpart to the west, East Germany was unable to recover from the ravages of war; poor social and economic conditions led to a failed uprising in 1953.
- Four million people emigrated to West Germany before the *Berlin Wall* was put up in 1961.
- Communism collapsed in 1989 and in October 1990 Germany was reunified after 45 years of division.

TIP Despite its misleading name, the German Democratic Republic was an undemocratic state that was under communist rule.

DS **General Strike, 1926:** a strike focusing on miners' grievances that was the climax to several years of industrial unrest in Britain.

- Since 1915, coal prices had fallen. Mine owners decided to cut miners' wages, a move that led the Miners' Federation to ask for the support of other trade unions.
- The strike lasted from 4 to 12 May and involved transport workers, builders, printers, workers in heavy industry and engineers.
- *Baldwin's Conservative* government was fully prepared to deal with the strike and used soldiers, policemen and volunteers to keep the country running.

TIP The General Strike left a deep wound and affected industrial relations between the trade unions and successive Conservative governments.

Geneva Accords, 1954: a peace agreement to determine the future of Vietnam that followed a Vietnamese victory in the 1945–54 war with France.

- Peace talks in Geneva involved the US, USSR, Britain, China, Laos, Cambodia and the competing Vietnamese regimes of *Ho Chi Minh* and Bao Dai.
- Vietnam was temporarily split along the line of the Seventeenth Parallel. The north became a communist republic and Bao Dai governed the south.
- The division was meant to mark a military truce line and not a permanent national border. The Geneva Accords planned for a nationwide election in 1956 but — fearing that widespread support for the communists in South Vietnam might lead to the entire country being communist controlled — the US and Bao Dai thwarted any democratic move to unification. Consequently, Vietnam remained a divided country.

TIP The USA's decision to oppose the accords led it to become directly interested and involved in the affairs of Vietnam. Eventual war with the communists lasted until 1973 and ended in US defeat.

Geneva Protocol, 1924: an attempt made by the British prime minister, Ramsay *MacDonald*, to strengthen the *League of Nations* (1920–45).

- MacDonald lost power later the same year and the new *Conservative* government did not sign the protocol.
- MacDonald backed arbitration by the Permanent Court of International Justice as the means to settle disputes between countries.

genocide: the extermination of a nationality or ethnic group on racial, religious or tribal grounds.

- The *Holocaust* represents the most extreme — but certainly not the only — example of twentieth-century genocide.

German Democratic Republic: see *GDR*.

DS **Gestapo:** the secret state police of the *Third Reich* (1933–45).

- The Gestapo was first and foremost a police force, but served primarily as an instrument of Nazi terror that helped the party maintain control of the state and the German people.
- In 1934 it was placed under the control of *Himmler* and the *SS*.

TIP An understanding of the Gestapo will help explain how the Nazi Party controlled the people of Germany as well as occupied Europe.

Giap, Vo Nguyen: a Vietnamese military leader who fought successful campaigns against the French (1946–54) and the US (1965–73).

- Giap's use of *guerrilla warfare* made him a leading architect of eventual communist victory in Vietnam.

DS ***glasnost*:** Russian for 'openness' and the word used to characterise *Gorbachev's* domestic policy and economic reforms.

- Along with *perestroika*, *glasnost* was adopted by Gorbachev to try to improve the *Soviet Union's* economic position.
- *Glasnost* allowed the Soviet people to say or write what they thought without being punished. This led to free elections in which many non-communists gained office.
- Gorbachev's hope that a freer Soviet people would try to make communism work proved false.

TIP *Glasnost* unwittingly and unintentionally contributed to the collapse of the Soviet Union.

DS ***Gleichschaltung*:** a German term to describe the forced coordination, or unification, of a country under Nazi rule.

- The main objective of *Gleichschaltung* was to create a centralised one-party state as quickly as possible.
- To do this the Nazis forced through a mass of legislation such as the *Enabling Act* (1933) that destroyed the last remnants of the German constitution and abolished opposition parties and independent labour unions.
- *Goebbels* brought all aspects of German culture, including the media, radio, music and journalism, under the control of the state.

TIP An understanding of *Gleichschaltung* is essential to explaining the Nazi takeover of Germany.

DS **Goebbels, Josef:** the Nazi propaganda minister (1933–45).

- Goebbels created and ran the Reich Ministry of Information and Propaganda in the first Nazi government. He encouraged the mass production of cheap radio sets to expand audiences for Nazi propaganda.
- In 1943, as the war started to turn against Germany, Goebbels called for *total war* and the full support of the German people.
- One day after *Hitler's* suicide, Goebbels poisoned his wife and children and shot himself.

TIP Goebbels's mastery of the techniques of mass communication was essential to the continuation of the Nazi state and the personality cult that surrounded Hitler.

DS **Golan Heights:** the high ground on the northeastern Israeli and southwestern Syrian frontier that is contested by both countries.

- The Golan Heights dominates much of northern Israel and the route to the Syrian capital, Damascus, and the terrain is strategically important to both sides.
- Israel occupied the Golan Heights following the 1967 *Arab–Israeli War.*
- In 1973 the Syrians temporarily regained control of the area during the Yom-Kippur War, but were driven off following the biggest tank battle since 1945.

TIP Israel's continued occupation of the Golan Heights remains a major obstacle to a lasting peace between it and Syria.

Gold Standard: a monetary system that uses gold to back a national currency by measuring its value against a fixed amount of the precious metal.

- The Gold Standard was a fundamental component of international trade before 1914, but suffered loss of confidence as part of the economic legacy of the *Great War* (1914–18).
- The standard was revised during the 1920s but was undermined by the *Depression.* In 1945 the US dollar was the world's leading trading currency and replaced the Gold Standard.

DS **Gorbachev, Mikhail:** leader of the Soviet Union (1985–91).

- Gorbachev recognised that the future of the Soviet Union depended on a significantly higher standard of living for its people. This led to *perestroika* (liberalising of politics) and *glasnost* (economic reform).
- He established a working relationship with President *Reagan* in the US, and in 1987 both leaders signed the INF Treaty.
- Gorbachev also engineered the Soviet withdrawal from *Afghanistan.*
- An attempted coup in 1991 failed to remove Gorbachev; but he resigned shortly after because the three leading republics of the USSR had already broken away and established the Commonwealth of Independent States under Boris *Yeltsin.*

TIP Gorbachev was a driving force behind the end of the *Cold War* (1945–91).

DS **Gosplan:** an abbreviation of the State Planning Commission, the Bolshevik economic planning body set up by *Lenin* in 1921.

- Gosplan was responsible for the *Five-Year Plans* and ran them from Moscow.
- Successive Soviet leaders used Gosplan until 1985, when *perestroika* allowed a greater degree of self-management in Soviet industry.

Greater East Asia Co-Prosperity Sphere: the Japanese name for the Asian countries it conquered between 1937 and 1942.

- The sphere included Malaya, the Philippines, eastern China and French Indo-China. These areas were rich in oil, tin and rubber, all of which were raw materials the Japanese mainland lacked.

DS **Great Leap Forward:** a Chinese communist slogan describing economic policies adopted in 1959.

- By the mid-1950s, Mao and other Chinese leaders decided Soviet methods were no longer appropriate for dealing with China's economic problems. This led them to reject the model issued by Moscow.
- The Chinese leadership aimed to build an industrial state by making full use of peasant communes formed in their own villages.
- Mao *Zedong* labelled the Great Leap Forward a 'short cut to communism'.

TIP After Mao distanced himself from Moscow, relations between China and the *Soviet Union* deteriorated and tension increased. This lasted over 30 years.

DS **Great Terror, 1928–53:** *Stalin's* campaign to eliminate all opposition to his rule.

- The Terror included: indiscriminate arrests, confessions obtained by torture, show trials, imprisonment without trial and mass executions.
- Millions of Soviet citizens from all walks of life fell victim to Stalin's paranoia. His purges of the *Red Army* between 1937 and 1941 contributed to the initial success of the German Operation *Barbarossa* (1941).
- The Terror came to an end in 1953 with Stalin's death.

TIP The sheer human scale and cost of Stalin's purges means that he rivals *Hitler* as the greatest mass murderer in human history.

Great War, 1914–18: a global military conflict that involved 31 countries and 65 million soldiers.

- Also known as the First World War or World War One, it was sparked by the assassination of *Franz Ferdinand* and fuelled by the *Alliance system*.
- The First World War was different from any earlier conflict in several ways: it was the first war where civilians were attacked; land-based fighting was widespread and took place in Europe, the Middle East and Africa; naval battles were fought all over the world.
- New technology and largely outdated strategy contributed to unprecedented slaughter and suffering. By the time the fighting ended on 11 November 1918, 13 million soldiers and 17 million civilians were dead and 20 million soldiers had been wounded.

TIP The Great War is a watershed in world history and a knowledge of it helps to explain the political, social and economic changes that came after 1918.

Guernica: a Spanish town bombed by German planes (*Luftwaffe*) during the *Spanish Civil War* (1936–39).

- The attack on Guernica took place for two reasons: firstly, to demonstrate German support for *Franco*; secondly, as a German experiment to observe the effects of an aerial attack on a defenceless population. Several hundred men, women and children were killed.
- Guernica was commemorated in Pablo Picasso's painting of the same name.

TIP International reporting of the attack intensified fears of massive civilian casualties in the event of another war.

guerrilla warfare: a type of warfare involving attacks by unconventional troops against an organised enemy.

- Guerrilla tactics include ambush, hit-and-run, sabotage and assassination.

TIP After 1945, guerrilla campaigns were the strategy of groups or political movements that faced numerically and technologically superior enemy forces.

DS ***Gulag:*** a system of forced-labour camps established by *Stalin* to house victims of the *Great Terror*.

- The camps were located primarily in Siberia and imprisoned the internal exiles of the *Soviet Union*.
- No one is sure exactly how many people were sent to the network of camps from the time it was established until the end of the Soviet regime; estimates range from 6 to 10 million prisoners.

DS **Guomindang:** the Chinese nationalist party founded by *Sun Yat Sen* that was devoted to political democracy and social reform.

- In 1921 the Chinese nationalist party established a government in southern China. Four years later, *Chiang* succeeded Sun Yat Sen.
- Throughout the 1930s, Guomindang led Chinese resistance to Japanese pressure and invasion. After the *Second World War* (1939–45), it launched a civil war against the Chinese communists.
- A communist victory forced it to retreat to the island of Taiwan (Formosa) and relations between the two groups have been tense ever since.

TIP The struggle between the Guomindang and the communists is the dominant feature of Chinese history during most of the twentieth century.

Haile Selassie: see *Abyssinian War*.

DS **Harding, Warren:** the US Republican president (1921–23) who wanted a 'return to normalcy' following the *Great War* (1914–18), but whose presidency is remembered as one of the most corrupt in US history.

- Harding quickly repealed many of the special powers given to the government during the war, including the war taxes his predecessor had introduced.
- His biggest mistake was to give important government jobs to many of those who helped him get elected. Many of these men subsequently used their power for personal gain.
- Harding's *foreign policy* was notable for the *Washington Conference* (1921–22) and a return to isolation.
- Betrayal by a few of the men he most trusted put a strain on Harding's health and he died suddenly in August 1923.

DS **Hawley–Smoot Tariff, 1930:** a law signed by *Hoover* to raise duties on foreign imports by about one-third.

- Hoover agreed to increased tariffs despite warnings from prominent economists.
- The tariff not only made it more difficult for debtor countries to earn the dollars necessary to repay US loans, but also goaded them into raising tariffs, thus harming international trade even further.

TIP
The Hawley–Smoot Tariff was a desperate policy that sent out the wrong messages, namely that the US was trying to be the world's banker, food producer and manufacturer whilst buying as little as possible in return.

hegemony: a position of unrivalled leadership or domination by one power within a group of states.

- The pursuit of economic or political hegemony is often the driving force behind a state's *foreign policy*.

DS **Henderson, Arthur:** a key figure in the rise of the British *Labour Party*.

- Henderson served in both *Asquith* and *Lloyd George* governments during the *Great War* (1914–18).
- Henderson was home secretary in the first Labour government (January–

October 1924) and foreign secretary in the second (1929–31).

- It was as foreign secretary that Henderson scored his greatest successes; he was a strong proponent of the *League of Nations* (1920–45), played a key role in the *Young Plan* (1929) and resumed diplomatic relations with the *Soviet Union*.
- In 1934 he was awarded the Nobel Peace Prize for efforts in support of *disarmament*.

TIP Henderson is credited with breaking Labour away from its traditional dependence on the Liberals and establishing it as a separate political party.

DS **Himmler, Heinrich:** commander of the *SS* (1925–45).

- Himmler saw the SS as a future German elite that would be the basis of guaranteed Aryan stock.
- Under him, the SS branched into several areas: espionage, running the concentration and death camps, military units fighting alongside the regular German army, serving in the *Einsatzgruppen*, and setting up a profitable economic section.
- Himmler was captured by the British in 1945 and committed suicide while being interrogated.

TIP Himmler's role and responsibility in carrying out the *Final Solution* are unquestioned; after *Hitler* he was, arguably, the most powerful man in Nazi Germany.

DS **Hindenburg, Paul von:** president of Germany (1925–34).

- Hindenburg fought for Prussia in 1866 and 1871, and during the First World War was commander of German armies on the Eastern Front and then chief of staff of all German armies.
- Hindenburg was appointed president of the ailing *Weimar Republic* in 1925. He was sympathetic to conservatives but opposed *National Socialism*.
- Despite assurances that he would never bring *Hitler* to power, Hindenburg appointed him chancellor in January 1933 after a strong showing by the Nazis in the April 1932 elections.

TIP Hindenburg was the last major obstacle in Germany to a Nazi dictatorship and his death in 1934 left Hitler unrestrained in his pursuit of total power.

Hirohito: emperor of Japan (1926–89).

- Before and during the *Second World War* (1939–45), Hirohito had a semi-divine status among his people. During this time, Japan followed an increasingly aggressive and expansionist *foreign policy*.
- After 1945, the new Japanese constitution classed Hirohito as a monarch who represented his people only.

TIP Hirohito's role and active participation in the growth of aggressive Japanese nationalism have been the subject of intense debate. *Cold War* (1945–91) politics made it undesirable for him to stand trial as an alleged war criminal.

Hiroshima: see *atomic bomb*.

Hitler, Adolf: the German *Führer* (total leader) of the *Third Reich* (1933–45).

- Hitler was born in Austria and served in the German army during the *Great War* (1914–18). He joined the Nazi Party in 1919 and became leader 2 years later.
- His political philosophy was a skewed worldview dictated by race, *capitalism, communism, nationalism* and *anti-Semitism*. He blamed Germany's post-1918 economic problems, as well as the war, on an international Jewish conspiracy and authorised the *Final Solution*.
- Hitler's first attempt to seize power was his failed *Beer Hall Putsch* (1923).
- He secured the German chancellorship in January 1933 following the *Depression* and created a dictatorship between 1933 and 1934.
- Hitler's policies were increasingly driven by his belief in the invincibility of his will. He wanted to build a thousand-year Reich (empire) enveloping all of Europe and, in particular, the *Soviet Union*.
- He survived an assassination attempt in July 1944 but committed suicide in Berlin in April 1945 as Soviet troops approached his bunker.

TIP Hitler is one of the most significant figures of the twentieth century. He was responsible for Germany's military defeat and the deaths of millions of people.

DS **Hitler Youth, 1926–45:** the Nazi Party organisation made compulsory for German boys aged between 15 and 18.

- This youth organisation provided a range of activities and military training with the aim of taking adolescents and turning them into indoctrinated Nazis.

TIP The Hitler Youth played a key role in the Nazi programme to control the German people.

Hoare–Laval Pact, 1935: see *Abyssinian War*.

Ho Chi Minh: Vietnamese nationalist, founder of the Communist Party in Indo-China, and president of North Vietnam, 1955–69.

- During the *Second World War* (1939–45), the USA backed Ho Chi Minh and the *Vietminh* in the struggle against occupying Japanese forces.
- In 1946 Ho Chi Minh continued the fight for Vietnamese independence when the French returned to govern their former colony.
- The defeat of the French in 1954 left the country divided into North and South, with Ho as North Vietnamese leader. He wanted to unite the country under communist control and was supported by the *Soviet Union* as well as China and southern Vietnamese communists (*Vietcong*).
- The US sent military supplies to the forces fighting Ho Chi Minh. In 1965 US combat troops began arriving in South Vietnam.

TIP Ho Chi Minh is a central figure in the Vietnamese struggle for independence, as well as the US policy of *containment*.

Holocaust: the systematic state-sponsored persecution of Jews and others by the

Nazi regime from 1933 to 1945 that culminated in the *Final Solution*. See also *Auschwitz*, *death camps* and *Einsatzgruppen*.

DS **Hoover, Herbert:** US Republican president (1929–33).

- Soon after Hoover took office, the US was in the grip of the *Wall Street Crash* and the *Depression*.
- Hoover believed it was the responsibility of private charities and businesses to get the US back on its feet. Thus, his term witnessed little government action to address the problem of unemployment. Instead, he relied on business as usual and waited for the Depression to wear itself out.
- Hoover backed *Hawley–Smoot* and, in 1931, set up the *Reconstruction Finance Corporation* to help banks and finance companies that were in danger of collapse.
- In the 1932 presidential election, *Roosevelt* overwhelmingly defeated Hoover.

Hungarian Uprising, 1956: a revolt against communist control in Hungary that was crushed by the *Red Army*.

- *Khrushchev's* suggestion that Moscow would tolerate different kinds of communism encouraged the Hungarians to announce multi-party elections and a withdrawal from the *Warsaw Pact*.
- Soviet tanks and soldiers were sent in against hopelessly outnumbered and outgunned Hungarian workers and students.
- The uprising demonstrated that *communism* could only be kept in place by force.

TIP Although the *Eisenhower* government encouraged Soviet-controlled countries to liberate themselves with US assistance, the US was unable to help the Hungarian rebels without igniting a world war.

hydrogen bomb: a weapon of mass destruction that heightened tension during the *Cold War* (1945–91).

- The US detonated the first hydrogen bomb in November 1952 and the Soviets followed suit several months later.
- The H-bomb had 2,500 times more explosive power than the first atom bomb.

TIP The introduction of the hydrogen bomb escalated the *arms race*.

hyperinflation: a period of rapid inflation marked by an escalating rise in prices and fall in the purchasing power of money.

- *Weimar* Germany was crippled by hyperinflation in 1923 when the government printed large amounts of money in an attempt to tackle its economic problems.
- This caused prices to rise and the faster prices went up, the faster people spent their wages. The savings of Germany's middle class and anyone living on fixed incomes were wiped out almost overnight.
- German hyperinflation ended when the *Stresemann* government abolished the mark (German currency) and replaced it with the *Rentenmark*.

TIP Hyperinflation caused political unrest in all parts of Germany and triggered the *Beer Hall Putsch* (1923).

ICBM: see *intercontinental ballistic missile.*

DS **immigration quotas:** these were limits set by the 1921 Immigration Act passed by the US *Congress.*

- The act stated that annual immigration of a given nationality could not exceed 3% of the number of immigrants from that nation residing in the US in 1910.
- It was a government attempt to stop the number of immigrants attracted by the *boom*. By 1929 the total of immigrants allowed into the US was reduced to 150,000 per year.
- The quotas favoured northern and western Europeans, in keeping with prejudices against immigrants from southern and eastern Europe.

TIP Immigration quotas marked the end of free immigration and the policy limiting particular races was criticised as a betrayal of everything the US stood for.

imperialism: the policy of a nation to acquire, administer and develop less materially developed territories or countries.

- Empires were built primarily to boost trade or prestige. They also alleviated overpopulation of the home country, supplied the need for new sources of raw materials and created markets for mass-produced goods.
- Many of the European powers supported imperialism during the late nineteenth and early twentieth centuries.
- Since 1918, imperialism has tended to take the form of economic domination rather than political intervention.

TIP Competition and tension between the imperial powers was a major cause of the *Great War* (1914–18).

Indo-China: the name given by France to its dependencies or colonies in Southeast Asia from 1887 to 1954.

- The main territories of Indo-China included Laos, Cambodia and Vietnam.
- French involvement in the region formally ended following the *Geneva Accords* (1954). However, independence failed to bring peace to any of these lands.

INF Treaty: see *Intermediate Nuclear Forces Treaty.*

integration: see *desegregation*.

intercontinental ballistic missile (ICBM): long-range nuclear-armed rockets developed by the US and the USSR during the 1950s.

- When the Soviets sent *Sputnik*, the first space satellite, to orbit the earth, US fears of a missile gap between the countries grew considerably.
- As the 1950s closed, the US had overwhelming strategic dominance because of its air–sea–land triad of long-range bombers, submarine-launched ballistic missiles (SLBMs), and ICBMs.
- By the late 1960s both sides had developed an anti-ballistic missile (ABM) system.

TIP The introduction of ICBMs heralded a dangerous new phase of the *Cold War* (1945–91); before 1957 both sides relied on relatively slow-moving bombers to deliver a nuclear attack.

Intermediate Nuclear Forces Treaty (INF), 1987: an agreement between *Gorbachev* and *Reagan* to ban land-based intermediate-range nuclear missiles in Europe.

- Medium and short-range missiles were designed to be used within a continent rather than between continents. Development of the US *Pershing II* and *Cruise* missiles and the Soviet *SS20* missile led to a cooling of *détente* at the start of the 1980s.
- The INF Treaty resulted in the destruction of 2,800 missiles. Gorbachev also unilaterally reduced his nation's armed forces.

TIP INF was an important step towards establishing better relations between the US and USSR. It also removed a significant threat to peace, for the presence of land-based intermediate-range nuclear missiles convinced some on both sides that a limited nuclear war was both possible and winnable.

International Brigades: the volunteers recruited by the communist parties of many European countries to fight during the *Spanish Civil War* (1936–39).

- Around 40,000 non-Spaniards fought with the International Brigades and more than a third were killed in action.
- Young foreigners were typically drawn to the conflict to stop the spread of *fascism*; many saw Spain as the first European battleground in a war between political ideologies.

TIP Italy, Germany and the *Soviet Union* sent weapons and men in support of one side or the other. The remaining European countries, most of which followed a policy of non-intervention, did not officially sanction the International Brigades.

DS ***intifada*:** the Arabic word for the full-scale uprising that erupted in 1987 against Israeli rule in the *West Bank* and *Gaza Strip*.

- To protest the Israeli occupation, thousands of Palestinians took to the streets, put up barricades and stoned Israeli army patrols.

- Israel's refusal to negotiate with the Palestinians led the US to reverse its policy and talk with PLO leaders after *Arafat* renounced terrorism.
- The Israeli response was a policy of beatings, shootings and confiscation of further Palestinian land; by 1991 over 1,000 Palestinians had been killed, over 2,000 homes destroyed and 15,000 people imprisoned.

DS **IRA:** see *Irish Republican Army*.

DS **Irish Free State:** the modern Irish state created by the Anglo-Irish treaty signed by the British prime minister, *Lloyd George*, and the Irish representative, Michael Collins.

- The Anglo-Irish treaty relaxed British rule over southern Ireland.
- It followed the Government of Ireland Act (1920) that established separate parliaments for the six northern counties (*Ulster*) and the rest of Ireland.
- The Republic of Ireland was established in 1949, when Britain formally accepted the independence of southern Ireland.

TIP The future of the six remaining northern counties has been the cause of ongoing political and military conflict.

DS **Irish Republican Army (IRA):** an armed organisation that has fought a *guerrilla* campaign in its struggle for Irish independence from Britain.

- Since 1921, the IRA has carried out numerous murders and bomb attacks.
- It is represented in negotiations by its political wing, Sinn Fein.
- Violence escalated in the early 1970s when extremists on both sides turned increasingly to *terrorism*.
- A cease-fire was declared in 1995, but did not hold.

DS **Irgun:** a Jewish organisation that fought for Jewish independence from 1945 to 1947.

- Irgun used *terrorism* against the British in *Palestine*. The group's worst atrocity was the 1946 destruction of the King David hotel in Jerusalem, which housed the British military headquarters.
- Irgun fought in support of *Zionism*. Many Jews believed the British were preventing the establishment of a Jewish state and they took up arms. Between 1945 and 1948, some 300 British servicemen and officials were murdered.

TIP The Irgun campaign was a major factor influencing the British decision to withdraw from Palestine in 1947.

Iron Curtain: the term used to describe the frontier that divided Eastern Europe from Western Europe during the *Cold War* (1945–91).

- The term was first used by *Goebbels* but was popularised by *Churchill* in a speech at Fulton, Missouri in 1946.
- By 1948, the Iron Curtain was a 2,000 kilometre stretch of barbed wire, sentry posts and blocked roads that dominated the political geography of post-1945 Europe.

TIP Churchill's remarks fed a growing belief among many US officials that only a tough approach would work with the *Soviet Union* and led to a deterioration of East–West relations.

isolationism: a policy of non-participation in, or withdrawal from, alliances with other countries or the affairs of other countries.

- Isolationism was the recurring theme of US *foreign policy* during the twentieth century. It played a role in the rejection of the international idealism of President *Wilson*.
- The policy was abandoned temporarily in 1917 when the US entered the *Great War* (1914–18); it returned during the interwar period only to be shattered by the Japanese attack on *Pearl Harbor* (1941).

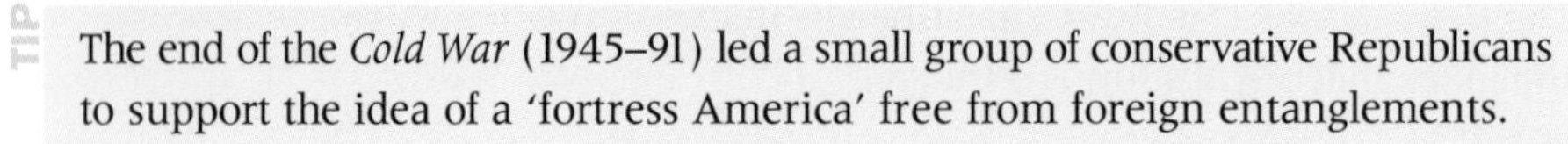

TIP The end of the *Cold War* (1945–91) led a small group of conservative Republicans to support the idea of a 'fortress America' free from foreign entanglements.

DS **Johnson, Lyndon:** the US Democratic president (1963–68) whose administration was marked by the *Vietnam War* (1946–75) and his declared 'war on poverty'.

- Johnson became president after *Kennedy's* assassination.
- His domestic policies brought about *civil rights* legislation, plus help for the unemployed, young urban Americans, the sick, the disabled and the elderly.
- In 1965 Johnson committed US ground troops to the conflict in Vietnam. Increased opposition to the war and the lack of a decisive military breakthrough helped persuade him not to stand for re-election in 1968.

TIP Johnson's war on poverty was one of the most ambitious initiatives by a US president.

Johnson Doctrine, 1965: President *Johnson's* declaration that the US would prevent 'another Cuba' by stopping communists from coming to power in the Western hemisphere.

- In 1965 Johnson dispatched 20,000 US troops to the Dominican Republic to prevent a socialist government from taking over.

TIP The doctrine reflected Johnson's ardent anti-communism as well as his commitment to global *containment*.

July Crisis, 1914: a European political crisis that resulted in the outbreak of the *Great War* (1914–18).

- The crisis was sparked by the assassination of *Franz Ferdinand*. His killing was quickly followed by an Austro-Hungarian declaration of war against *Serbia*.
- The *Alliance system* and the need to mobilise armies forced the leaders of the European powers to make rapid decisions. The German *Schlieffen Plan* brought war with Britain.

TIP The July Crisis brought to a climax growing international tension over naval, colonial and economic rivalries that had intensified since the turn of the century.

j

DS **July Days, 1917:** a period of political and social unrest used by *Lenin* and the Bolsheviks to attempt a seizure of power in Russia.

- In May and June 1917, *Kerensky* prepared the Russian army for an offensive against the Austrians in order to gain support for the *Provisional Government* (1917). Meanwhile, Lenin built up his party's power base.
- Against Lenin's wishes, Bolshevik supporters joined armed soldiers and sailors and took to the streets. The authorities responded by arresting Bolshevik leaders and Lenin was forced into hiding.

TIP The *Kornilov Affair* (1917) helps explain the Bolsheviks' rapid recovery from the July Crisis.

DS **July Plot, 1944:** an attempt by anti-Nazi groups in Germany to overthrow *Hitler* and secure peace with Britain and the USA.

- A bomb was left at Hitler's conference table in his headquarters in East Prussia.
- Hitler was only wounded, and with no plans in place to cut communications between Hitler and his supporters in Berlin, the conspiracy failed.
- The Nazis took savage reprisals on the alleged conspirators and Hitler purged the German army.

TIP The July Plot was the most serious of several attempts to assassinate Hitler.

DS **Jutland, Battle of, 1916:** a naval engagement between the British Grand Fleet and the German High Seas Fleet.

- The battle was a series of actions from the afternoon of 31 May to the early hours of the following day.
- The British lost 14 vessels to the Germans' 13. At the end of the battle the remaining German ships returned to port, making the outcome indecisive.

TIP Since the German fleet never again dared to seek out the Royal Navy, but instead chose to remain in harbour, Jutland is generally seen as a British victory.

DS **Kaiser:** see *William II.*

DS **Kapp Putsch, 1920:** a right-wing conspiracy in Germany to overthrow the *Weimar Republic.*

- A brigade of the *Freikorps* marched into Berlin in protest at the government's acceptance of the Treaty of *Versailles* (1919). The intention was to install Wolfgang Kapp as chancellor.
- A general strike of workers demonstrated there was little popular support for the putsch. This, and the refusal of the German army to back the rebels, led to its collapse after 5 days.

TIP The Kapp Putsch revealed the power and the political sympathies of the *Freikorps.*

Kellogg–Briand Pact, 1928: an international agreement to renounce war as an instrument of *foreign policy.*

- The pact started as a bilateral agreement between the US and France. It was named after Frank Kellogg, the US secretary of state and the French foreign minister, Aristide Briand.
- Kellogg wanted wider inclusion and eventually 65 countries joined. Even though they were not members of the *League of Nations* (1920–45), the US, Germany and the USSR signed the pact.

TIP While the Kellogg–Briand Pact was seen as a significant step towards the peaceful resolution of international conflict, it contained no provision for punishing aggressors and lacked real authority.

Kemal, Mustafa (Ataturk): the founder of the modern Turkish state.

- In April 1920 he set up a provisional government in Ankara and secured a revision of the Treaty of *Sevres* (1920) by the Treaty of *Lausanne* (1923).
- He established a republic in Turkey in 1923, and led a non-religious and westernised industrial state until his death.

TIP Ataturk's rule marks the turning away of Turkish identity from the Islamic loyalties of its past toward a more European outlook.

DS **Kennedy, John (JFK):** the US Democratic president (1961–63) whose administration was dominated by international relations and *foreign policy.*

- JFK aimed to improve the daily lives of ordinary US citizens through his *New Frontier* laws, but his social reform programme was stalled in *Congress* by an alliance of Republicans and southern Democrats.
- A strong believer in the *domino theory,* Kennedy was involved with the *Bay of Pigs* (1961), the *Cuban Missile Crisis* (1962), the *Berlin Wall* (1962) and the *Nuclear Test Ban Treaty* (1963).
- President Kennedy was assassinated on 22 November 1963 in Dallas, Texas.

TIP Kennedy was in office during one of the most dangerous and difficult periods of the *Cold War* (1945–91).

DS **Kerensky, Alexander:** Russian revolutionary leader of the *Provisional Government* (1917).

- Kerensky was a member of the *Duma.* After the *February Revolution* (1917) he became war minister and prime minister.
- He made the mistake of trying to continue Russian involvement in the *Great War* (1914–18), a move that went against the tide of popular feeling in his country.
- The *Kornilov Affair* (1917) undermined Kerensky's position and he was forced from office in the *October Revolution of 1917.*

TIP An understanding of Kerensky's leadership helps explain the failure of the Provisional Government.

DS **KGB:** one of the secret police forces of the *Soviet Union.*

- The KGB was responsible for state security including political trials, internal exile, censorship, espionage and executions. It administered the *Gulag.*
- The KGB also worked around the world to help establish and support pro-Soviet governments.

DS **Khrushchev, Nikita:** the Soviet leader (1955–64) whose policy of *destalinisation* led to domestic reforms and *peaceful coexistence* with the West.

- In 1956 Khrushchev condemned *Stalin* and his policies.
- His own domestic policies focused on improving agriculture and industry. He did this by moving towards more decentralised economic management.
- Khrushchev's *foreign policy* failures led to his downfall. He helped establish the *Warsaw Pact* (1955), ordered his military to crush the *Hungarian Uprising* (1956) and was the first to back down during the *Cuban Missile Crisis* (1962).

TIP Despite helping to ease the threat of *nuclear war,* Khrushchev's legacy in Soviet history is one of weakness and failure.

DS **Kiel Mutiny, 1918:** the climax of civil unrest involving hundreds of German seamen who were dissatisfied with political leadership in the *Great War* (1914–18).

- As the First World War wound down, the German government ordered the German fleet to mount a suicide attack on the Royal Navy. Few sailors were prepared to throw away their lives and they rebelled.
- In a move that reminded many of what happened in Russia in 1917, groups of German soldiers and workers joined the sailors to take over key cities and towns throughout the country. This revolution persuaded the Kaiser to abdicate.

TIP The November Revolution (1918) led to the *armistice* and the first appearance of parliamentary democracy in Germany.

Kim Il Sung: communist leader (1945–94) of North Korea.

- After the *Second World War* (1939–45), Russian troops occupied North Korea. During the *Cold War* (1945–91), the division of Korea became permanent.
- Kim allied his country with the USSR. In 1950, he started the *Korean War* (1950–53).
- His emphasis on self-reliance kept North Korea dependent on hard-line communism and isolated from much of the world. Following Kim's death in 1994 his son Kim Jong Il took over.

TIP During nearly 50 years as ruler, Kim Il Sung fostered a powerful cult of personality that helped him stay in power.

DS **King, Martin Luther:** an African–American Baptist minister and *civil rights* leader who was committed to non-violent protest.

- In 1957 he became the first president of the Southern Christian Leadership Conference, which was established to coordinate civil rights activities.
- King was instrumental in the *Montgomery Bus Boycott* (1955–56), led marches and demonstrations against *segregation* and won the Nobel Peace Prize in 1964.
- He was assassinated in 1968.

TIP King's movement for peaceful protest helped to change the attitudes of millions of white Americans towards African–Americans and he remains the central figure in the struggle for black civil rights in America.

DS **Kissinger, Henry:** a German-born political scientist who served as national security adviser (1969–73) and secretary of state (1973–77) under President *Nixon*.

- Kissinger followed a strategy designed to promote a global *balance of power* through *détente*.
- He negotiated trade relations with the *Soviet Union*, helped to slow the *arms race*, and restored relations with China in 1972.
- In 1973 he signed a cease-fire with North Vietnam that led to US withdrawal from the *Vietnam War* (1946–75).
- Shuttle diplomacy had him flying repeatedly between Middle East capitals in search of an Arab–Israeli peace settlement.

DS **KKK:** see *Ku Klux Klan*.

DS ***kolkhoz:*** see *collectivisation.*

Korean War, 1950–53: the first major military conflict of the *Cold War* (1945–91).

- The invasion of South Korea by communist North Korea was the climax of 5 years of clashes along the supposedly temporary border that separated the two countries.
- The *United Nations* authorised the use of force to remove the North Koreans; 15 nations including Britain and France sent troops to fight under US command.
- By 1951 the fighting had stabilised around the original border but *armistice* talks did not take place for another 2 years.

TIP The war resulted in the entrenchment of military *containment* as US policy.

DS **Kornilov Affair, 1917:** a revolt of the Russian army commander-in-chief that seriously undermined the *Provisional Government* (1917).

- Confident he had the backing of *Kerensky* to reorganise and strengthen the Provisional Government, General Kornilov moved to destroy the Petrograd *soviet.*
- Kerensky believed that Kornilov was planning to seize power himself; to defeat him, Kerensky was forced to release several Bolshevik leaders from jail and rely on their support.

TIP The episode demonstrated how Kerensky had lost the support of the army and was powerless to prevent the Bolsheviks from building their support in the Russian countryside, towns and factories.

DS ***Kristallnacht*, 1938:** a night of Nazi persecution of Jews throughout much of Germany.

- Following the murder in Paris of a German official by a Polish Jew, the *SS* organised riots against German Jews.
- In one November night at least 74 Jews were murdered, 20,000 arrested and hundreds of buildings were destroyed. To pay for the damage, Germany's Jews were heavily fined and their property was confiscated.

TIP *Kristallnacht* marked the transition of Nazi *anti-Semitism* from isolated attacks to the start of a national state-sanctioned policy that ended with the *Final Solution.*

DS **Kronstadt Mutiny, 1921:** a revolt by Russian sailors against *war communism.*

- Anger at the hardships and increasing violence used by the Bolsheviks to control the workers and peasants led the sailors to take over their naval base and demand greater freedoms.
- The *Red Army,* under *Trotsky's* leadership, crushed the revolt.

TIP The mutiny convinced *Lenin* of two key points: firstly, that war communism was a failure (he replaced it with the *New Economic Policy*); secondly, that he needed to centralise power within the party.

DS **Ku Klux Klan (KKK):** a secret, anti-black, anti-Catholic and anti-Semitic society in the US that was founded to advance white supremacy in the Southern states.

- The KKK was originally established in 1866 to terrorise freed slaves.
- Although formally disbanded 3 years later, it reappeared in 1915 and was particularly active between 1922 and 1930.

TIP The height of Klan activity in the 1920s can be linked to the strong anti-international and isolationist sentiment in the USA at that time.

DS ***kulak*:** the former peasants in Russia who prospered under *Stolypin's* agrarian reforms.

- The Bolsheviks opposed Stolypin's goal of a stable middle class built around the *kulaks*.
- The *kulak* class vigorously resisted *collectivisation* and, as a result, was all but wiped out by *Stalin*.

TIP The fate of the *kulaks* is closely linked to the first *Five-Year Plan*.

Kursk, Battle of, 1943: a tank battle during the *Second World War* (1939–45) that marked the end of the German offensive against the *Soviet Union*.

- Over 2,700 German vehicles and a million men failed to overwhelm the Russian army situated in and around the city of Kursk.

TIP This battle and the Battle of *Stalingrad* (1942–43) marked the turning points on the Eastern Front; after 1943 the Germans were on the defensive for the remainder of the war.

DS **Labour Party:** originally a British socialist political organisation.

- The roots of the Labour Party go back to 1900 and the Labour Representation Committee (LRC), an association of various socialist groups. *MacDonald* was the first LRC secretary.
- The *Lloyd George* War Cabinet gave party members Labour's first government experience. In 1922, Labour became the main opposition party.
- A year later it formed a short-lived minority government before returning to office in 1929. Its first sustained taste of power came after 1945 when *Attlee* introduced the *welfare state* to Britain.
- In 1997 a reformed party with the title 'New Labour' achieved a landslide victory in the general election under Tony Blair. Blair was re-elected in 2001.

TIP Knowledge of the Labour Party's rise to power is important for an understanding of twentieth-century British political history.

Lateran Treaties, 1928: an agreement between *Mussolini* and the papacy that ended 50 years of friction between the Italian state and church.

- The treaties recognised the Vatican as an independent state and Catholicism as the only state religion. In addition to establishing compulsory religious education in Italian schools, the state paid the church an indemnity for land lost in 1861.
- In return, the pope accepted the king and Mussolini as rulers of Italy.

TIP Mussolini recognised the importance of papal endorsement to his rule; the treaties made him more respectable and persuaded many loyal Catholics to support *fascism*.

Latvia: one of the three *Baltic States*.

- Before the *Great War* (1914–18), Latvia was part of Russia. After 1918, it became an independent republic (1918–40). It was then occupied by the Russians for the next 50 years until again declaring its independence in 1991.

Lausanne, Treaty of, 1923: the peace treaty between Turkey and the Allies that replaced the Treaty of *Sevres* (1920).

- Following the *Chanak Crisis* (1922), the Turkish leader *Kemal* mounted a

successful challenge to Sevres and won back much of the land Turkey had lost, including eastern Thrace and Smyrna. It also regained control of the Black Sea Straits.

- Over a million Greeks living in Turkey were forced to leave their homes and some 400,000 Turks left Greece.

TIP

Kemal's refusal to consider the Treaty of Sevres as binding, and its subsequent replacement by the Treaty of Lausanne, demonstrated that the *Paris Peace Treaties* (1919–20) could be challenged successfully.

League of Nations, 1920–45: an international organisation established to preserve peace and settle disputes by negotiation and arbitration.

- President *Wilson* made formation of the League of Nations one of his *Fourteen Points*.
- Because *Congress* refused to ratify (make into law) the Treaty of *Versailles* (1919), the US was never a member. Germany belonged from 1926 to 1933 and the *Soviet Union* from 1934 to 1939.
- The League of Nations lacked an armed force to coerce aggressive member states but instead relied on *sanctions*. This weakness thwarted its ability to keep peace during the 1930s.
- It did have some success in mediating conflict between smaller states and in addressing refugee problems.

TIP

Questions on the League of Nations often focus on the issue of whether or not it was doomed to fail from the start.

DS ***Lebensraum*:** German for 'living space' and the slogan of German expansionism that was a major aim of *Hitler's foreign policy*.

- Hitler believed Germany was overpopulated and needed more farmland to support itself. He maintained that the *Lebensraum* beyond Germany's borders was populated by what he called 'minor nations' and 'inferior races'.
- The doctrine of *Lebensraum* and a hatred of communism were Hitler's main reasons for launching Operation *Barbarossa* (1941).

TIP

Lebensraum made war between Germany and the *Soviet Union* inevitable. The idea is closely linked to *autarky*.

lend–lease: a term derived from *Roosevelt's* Lend–Lease Act that made it possible to provide military supplies to Britain and its allies.

- Roosevelt wanted to find a way to support Britain while also calming the fears of those in his country who wanted the US to stay out of the *Second World War* (1939–45).
- Roosevelt regarded the US as the 'great arsenal of democracy' and by the end of the war Britain had received over $31 billion worth of military goods. Ownership of these remained in US hands and payment was either deferred until after the war or cancelled in return for US use of British military bases.

TIP It was part of Roosevelt's strategy to move his nation from neutrality to undeclared war against Germany and then to full-scale war itself.

DS **Lenin, Vladimir:** the leader of the Russian Communist Party and founder of the *Soviet Union*.

- In 1903 Lenin led the militant wing of the Russian Social Democrats, or Bolshevik faction.
- Lenin seized power form the *Provisional Government* in October 1917 and carried through a major distribution of land and the *nationalisation* of the banks and property.
- His attempts to achieve a communist economic revolution led to *war communism* and then the *New Economic Plan*.

TIP Lenin was responsible for the creation of the communist state in the Soviet Union.

liberalism: a term given to a set of beliefs that favour moderate reform, social and political progress and individual freedom.

- The roots of liberalism are found in the eighteenth and nineteenth centuries.

DS **Liberal Party:** a British political party that was one of the two major parties until overtaken by the *Labour Party*.

- The Liberals were the successors to the Whigs.
- The party traditionally advocated a pacific attitude towards foreign and imperial affairs, free trade economics and political reform.
- The Liberal Party was damaged by the dispute between *Asquith* and *Lloyd George* during the *Great War* (1914–18). Since then the party has failed to secure an electoral majority.

TIP Until 1922 the Liberal Party was a major force in British politics.

DS **Liebknecht, Karl:** a German who jointly led the German Communist Party, or Spartacists, with Rosa *Luxemburg*.

- Spartacists were opposed to *Weimar* democracy and wanted to make Germany a communist state like Russia.
- In January 1919 the German Communist Party launched the *Spartacist Uprising* to seize power in Berlin.

TIP Spartacist actions demonstrated that German postwar democracy was unstable from its birth.

Lithuania: the southernmost of the three *Baltic States* created in 1918.

- The capital, Vilna, was the scene of ongoing Polish–Russian conflict. The Poles captured it in 1914 and held the city for 20 years.
- In 1923 the Lithuanians seized the predominantly German port of Memel, an act that later served as a rallying cry for support of *Hitler*. In 1939 the Germans occupied Memel.

- The *Soviet Union* absorbed Lithuania in 1940 and it remained under Moscow's control until it declared independence in 1990 along with Latvia and Estonia.

Little Entente, 1921: a system of alliances between Czechoslovakia, Romania and Yugoslavia (1920–21) intended to preserve the terms of the Treaties of *Saint-Germain* (1919) and *Trianon* (1920).

- The years 1929–37 witnessed increasing cooperation between the three countries that wanted to prevent Hungary from attempting to recover any territory.
- The Little Entente did not respond to the rising threat of *Hitler*, and once the British and French had abandoned Czechoslovakia in 1938, it collapsed and was formally abolished in 1939.

TIP The entente was ineffective at the moment of crisis and did little to challenge German aggression.

DS **Lloyd George, David:** British Liberal and prime minister (1916–22) who led his country to victory in the *Great War* (1914–18).

- Lloyd George began his career as a radical Liberal and was responsible for a series of social reforms including old age pensions and progressive taxation.
- In July 1915 he joined the *coalition government* under *Asquith* and then combined with the Conservatives a year later to overthrow Asquith.
- Lloyd George signed the *Paris Peace Treaties* (1919–20) despite presenting a moderate position towards Germany.
- After the war he achieved a settlement of the Irish problem through negotiations that led ultimately to the creation of the *Irish Free State*.

TIP Lloyd George's wartime leadership was crucial to a country that had tired of military stalemate and the rising cost of the conflict.

Locarno, Treaty of, 1925: an international agreement confirming the territorial changes made to Germany by the Treaty of *Versailles* (1919).

- France, Germany and Belgium agreed on the inviolability of the Franco-German and Belgo-German borders and demilitarisation of the Rhineland.
- The treaties paved the way for Germany to join the *League of Nations* (1920–45) in 1926.

TIP *Hitler* broke the Treaty of Locarno in 1936 when he remilitarised the *Rhineland*. The other signatories, then preoccupied with the *Abyssinian War* (1935–36), limited their response to formal protests.

London, Treaty of, 1915: a secret agreement made by the *Triple Entente* powers and Italy in order to convince Italy to become an allied belligerent in the *Great War* (1914–18).

- Convinced that Italian intervention would lead to a quick collapse of Austria–Hungary and 'open the back door to Germany', the Western powers offered significant territorial compensation to the Italians in return.

TIP The British and French turned against Italy at the *Paris Peace Treaties* (1919–20) and Italy received significantly less than it expected.

DS **Long March, 1934–35:** the retreat of Mao *Zedong* and about 100,000 of his followers as they fled the *Guomindang*.

- The Chinese communists trekked more than 6,000 miles over the course of several months, facing daily attacks as they crossed inhospitable terrain. Only about 20,000 survived the ordeal.
- At the end of the Long March, the communists established a new base and continued to resist until 1937, when they signed a truce with the Guomindang to face increasing Japanese aggression.

TIP For many decades the Long March stood as a symbol of communist heroism to those Chinese opposed to the Guomindang.

DS **Ludendorff, Erich:** a German soldier during the *Great War* (1914–18) who attached himself to extreme anti-republican groups and took part in both the *Kapp Putsch* (1920) and the *Beer Hall Putsch* (1923).

- Ludendorff was tried with *Hitler* and found not guilty of treason. He stood unsuccessfully as a Nazi presidential candidate in the 1925 election, earning less than 1% of the vote.

TIP Ludendorff's reputation as a soldier led to the rise of military influence in German civil affairs after the First World War.

DS ***Lusitania*:** the British passenger liner torpedoed and sunk off the Irish coast without warning by the German submarine *U-20* in May 1915.

- Over 100 of the 1,200 fatalities were US civilians. The loss of life caused widespread anger in the US.
- The Germans claimed the *Lusitania* was carrying war materials and was therefore a legitimate target.

TIP The sinking of the *Lusitania* and the *Zimmerman Telegram* (1917) help explain US entry into the *Great War* (1914–18).

DS **Luxemburg, Rosa:** a German revolutionary who helped lead the *Spartacist Uprising* (1919).

- Luxemburg took part in the *October Revolution of 1905* and joined *Liebknecht* as leaders of the German Spartacist League.
- They founded the German Communist Party (KPD) in 1918.
- During the Spartacist Uprising, Luxemburg and Liebknecht were murdered by the *Freikorps*.

DS **MacDonald, James Ramsay:** British prime minister (1924, 1929–35).

- MacDonald was key to the early organisation and establishment of the *Labour Party*.
- MacDonald's first stint as prime minister was largely undermined by the controversy surrounding the *Zinoviev* Letter but he was again elected in 1929.
- In 1931 his government split during the worsening financial and economic situation and he formed the *National Government*, which the majority of his party refused to support. MacDonald resigned in 1935 after 4 years as a figurehead for a predominantly Conservative administration.

TIP MacDonald was a leading figure in the attempt to establish *socialism* in Britain during the early part of the twentieth century.

MAD: see *Mutually Assured Destruction*.

Maginot Line: the line of fortifications built in the 1930s along the eastern border of France to protect against German attack.

- André Maginot, the French war minister, ordered construction of the defences that took his name. He based the French defence strategy on his experiences during the Battle of *Verdun* (1916).
- Belgian opposition and the French belief that the Germans could not go through the Ardennes forest meant the line was halted at the Franco-Belgian border.
- In 1940, German forces outflanked the Maginot Line with a *blitzkrieg* attack.

TIP French faith in the Maginot Line and the German tactical response is a testament to post-1918 French and German interpretations of lessons learned from the *Great War* (1914–18) and how these influenced each side's interwar military planning.

Manchuria: a region of northeast China conquered by the Japanese in 1931–32 as part of imperial expansion in East Asia.

- Japan wanted Manchurian coal and iron ore, so the Japanese military faked an incident between Chinese and Japanese soldiers at *Mukden* as an excuse to invade and conquer the interior, renaming it Manchukuo.

- The *League of Nations* (1920–45) sent the Lytton Commission to investigate the incident. Japan's response to the commission's condemnation of its actions was to leave the league in 1933.

TIP The Japanese invasion revealed the powerlessness of the League of Nations in the face of determined aggression. It also raised the prestige of the Japanese military and made it possible for the army to pressurise the civilian government into further imperial expansion.

mandates: the former colonies of the defeated German and Turkish empires after the *Great War* (1914–18).

- The *Paris Peace Treaties* (1919–20) ceded the territories to the victors but they remained the overall responsibility of the *League of Nations* (1920–45).
- It was intended that some mandates were to receive independence at an early stage, while others were seen as needing longer administration.

TIP For many of the colonial peoples, the treaties merely replaced one set of imperial rulers with another.

DS **Mandela, Nelson:** the *African National Congress* leader who became South Africa's first black president in 1994.

- Mandela was jailed from 1962 to 1990 for his campaign against *apartheid* and for a democratic multiracial South Africa.
- Upon his release, he negotiated the establishment of a multiracial government.

TIP Mandela is a key figure in the dismantling of apartheid in South Africa and the introduction of *democracy* to the country.

Mao Zedong: see *Zedong, Mao*.

DS **March Offensive, 1918:** a German attack on the *Western Front* that gambled for victory in a knockout blow.

- Victory in the Eastern Front, the Treaty of *Brest–Litovsk* (1918) and fear over the full impact of US troops convinced the German High Command to launch an all-or-nothing offensive against British and French troops.
- The attack was halted outside Paris by Allied troops — including newly arrived US reinforcements — at the second Battle of the *Marne* (1918).

TIP The March Offensive was Germany's last desperate attempt to snatch victory. Its failure saw the Germans forced onto the retreat until the November *armistice* was signed.

March on Rome, 1922: the fascist-inspired legend of the way *Mussolini* took power in Italy.

- Mussolini wanted to take advantage of the civil unrest that existed in Italy during 1922 after the fascists had helped break down a general workers' strike.
- In response to Mussolini's call to overthrow the government, thousands of fascist supporters moved towards Rome in October.

- Victor Emmanuel III, the Italian king, gave in to the fascists and appointed Mussolini as prime minister.

TIP Although Mussolini threatened violence if he did not get what he wanted, it is important to remember that he was handed power rather than seizing it.

DS **March on Washington, 1963:** a demonstration by supporters of African–American civil rights to put pressure on President *Kennedy* and the US *Congress* to pass laws making all forms of discrimination in public places illegal.

- Over 250,000 people — black and white — marched to the US capital and gathered at the Lincoln Memorial to hear Martin Luther *King* deliver his 'I have a dream' speech.

TIP The demonstration and speech were landmark events in the struggle for equity and justice; a year later President *Johnson* got Congress to pass the *Civil Rights Act*.

Marne battles, 1914, 1918: two significant Allied victories on the *Western Front* during the *Great War* (1914–18).

- In the first battle (1914) the French thwarted the *Schlieffen Plan* and prevented the capture of Paris.
- The second Battle of the Marne (1918) saw British, French and US troops halt the German *March Offensive*.

TIP Both battles were turning points in history; the first led to *trench warfare* and the second to Germany's surrender.

Marshall Aid: a US programme to provide financial assistance to help the European countries recover from the *Second World War* (1939–45).

- Between 1947 and 1952, $13 billion worth of food, vehicles and fuel flowed into Western Europe.
- Although the offer of aid was open to all countries, *Stalin* never allowed any East European country to take part.

TIP Marshall Aid was a key component of *containment*, which strengthened Western Europe against the threat of *communism*.

Marx, Karl: a German social philosopher and revolutionary who founded modern *socialism* and *communism*.

- Marx despised *capitalism*, which he believed created prosperity for a few and poverty for many. He called for an international struggle to bring about its downfall.
- In the *Communist Manifesto*, Marx set out his argument that history was a fight between the industrialists and middle class, or bourgeoisie, and the industrial workers, or proletariat.
- According to Marx, workers' revolutions would lead to the triumph of the proletariat and the creation of a socialist and egalitarian society in Western Europe.

TIP Revolutionaries around the world adapted Marxist ideas to their own ends and Marx had a massive influence on the course of twentieth-century history.

Marxism: see *Marx.*

Matteoti Affair, 1924: see *Acerbo Law.*

DS **Means Test:** a *National Government* policy to limit unemployment payments as part of spending cuts to tackle the international economic crisis (1929–31).

- Rising unemployment led to less government income from taxation and increased expenditure on unemployment benefit.
- The Means Test took a claimant's total family income and savings into account when deciding the level of unemployment benefit. Those who had been careful and saved received less benefit than those without any means at all.

TIP The Means Test was a divisive policy that further demoralised the unemployed. Working people hated it and many Labour-controlled local councils refused to administer it.

DS ***Mein Kampf*:** literally 'My Struggle', *Hitler's* book that set out his political ambitions.

- Hitler dictated the book to Rudolf Hess while both men were imprisoned (1924–25) following the failed *Beer Hall Putsch* (1923).
- *Mein Kampf* records Hitler's belief in the superiority of the Aryan race, his *anti-Semitism,* his dream of *Lebensraum* and his hatred of the Treaty of *Versailles* (1919).

TIP Historians have argued over whether *Mein Kampf* was the starting point for all Nazi policies or a crude general statement of Hitler's many prejudices.

DS **Menshevik:** the moderate faction of the Russian Social Democrat Party and rival to the Bolsheviks.

- Leading members of the party met in London in 1903 and split over issues of membership, leadership and political direction. The Mensheviks, led by *Trotsky,* wanted a mass-membership socialist party, while the Bolsheviks demanded that only a hard core of committed revolutionaries be included.
- *Lenin* played a key role in the split and emerged as leader of the Bolsheviks.
- The Mensheviks supported the *Provisional Government* (1917) and opposed the *October Revolution of 1917.* In 1922 Lenin banned the Mensheviks as a political organisation.

TIP The Mensheviks favoured a more democratic form of leadership, which put them in tune with other European socialist movements of the time.

Molotov–Ribbentrop Pact: see *Nazi–Soviet Pact.*

Mons, Battle of, 1914: the first battle fought by the *British Expeditionary Force* against the advancing Germans.

- The *Schlieffen Plan* had already met with stiff Belgian resistance before the Germans unexpectedly found themselves facing British forces.

- Heavy fighting took a terrible toll on both sides before the outnumbered British were forced to withdraw.

TIP While the BEF suffered high casualties, they delayed the Germans enough to thwart the Schlieffen Plan.

DS **Montgomery Bus Boycott, 1955–56:** a watershed event in the US civil rights struggle which brought Martin Luther *King* to national prominence.

- When Rosa Parks, a black woman, was arrested for refusing to give up her seat to a white man on a public bus in Montgomery, Alabama, local black groups decided to boycott the city's bus system.
- Adhering to King's policy of non-violent protest, African–Americans brought the bus company to the verge of bankruptcy and forced it to agree to *desegregation*.
- When a few white people turned to violence, the black protestors took their case to the courts; in 1956 the *Supreme Court* declared segregated buses unconstitutional.

TIP The boycott was a great victory for the civil rights movement. After 1955, King devoted his life to the campaign for civil equity and justice.

DS **moonshine:** see *bootlegger.*

Moroccan Crisis, 1905–06: see *Agadir.*

DS **Mubarak, Hosni:** the Egyptian president since 1981.

- Mubarak came to power after *Sadat* was assassinated in 1981 and continued Sadat's moderate pro-Western policies.

Mukden Incident, 1931: see *Manchuria.*

Munich Agreement, 1938: a settlement over the major international crisis involving the German, Italian, British, French and German leaders.

- The British prime minister, *Chamberlain*, and the French leader, Daladier, ceded the German-speaking *Sudetenland* of Czechoslovakia to Germany. Poland and Hungary also acquired territory at the expense of the Czechs, who were not consulted.
- The Munich crisis and subsequent agreement marked the climax of British and French *appeasement* of *Hitler*; when German troops marched unopposed into the remainder of Czechoslovakia in March 1939, the countdown to the *Second World War* (1939–45) began.

TIP Historians are divided over the Munich Agreement. Its defenders argue that it gave the West a vital year to improve military preparedness; critics reply that the British and French failed to seize a real opportunity to unite with the Czechs and make a powerful military alliance against Hitler.

DS **Munich Putsch, 1923:** see *Beer Hall Putsch.*

Mussolini, Benito: the Italian fascist leader (*Il Duce*) who ruled as prime minister (1922–43).

- Originally he was a socialist, but Mussolini's experiences as a soldier in the *Great War* (1914–18) made him exchange his belief in class struggle for an intense *nationalism.* He founded the Italian Fascist Party in 1919 as an anti-democratic and anti-socialist organisation.
- Mussolini came to power following the *March on Rome* (1922) and established a fascist dictatorship, loosely termed a *corporate state.*
- Mussolini embarked on an expansionist *foreign policy,* beginning with the *Abyssinian War* (1935–36). He moved closer to *Hitler* in 1936 and declared war on Britain and France in 1940.
- Italy's participation in the *Second World War* (1939–45) was disastrous; Allied forces invaded Italy in 1943 and Mussolini was forced to resign. He was captured and executed by Italian communists in 1945 while trying to escape to Switzerland.

TIP Mussolini's rise to power served as a model for politically ambitious strongmen elsewhere in Europe and was the inspiration for Hitler's *Beer Hall Putsch* (1923).

Mutually Assured Destruction (MAD): the belief shared in the *Soviet Union* and the US during the *Cold War* (1945–91) that a full-scale nuclear war between *superpowers* would result in unprecedented death and destruction and annihilate both sides.

DS **My Lai:** a Vietnamese village that was the scene of the worst atrocity against civilians committed by US troops during the *Vietnam War* (1946–75).

- US troops entered the village at the height of the *Tet Offensive* (1968) to look for *Vietcong* soldiers.
- The troops murdered between 300 and 500 men, women and children.
- Only one US soldier was convicted of murder following an investigation; he served 3 years of a life sentence before *Nixon* pardoned him.

TIP The My Lai massacre further polarised a nation that was already deeply divided over the war and caused many to question the US role in the conflict.

Nagasaki: see *atomic bomb*.

Nagy, Imre: the Hungarian prime minister (1953–55, 1956) whose challenge to Russian control of Eastern Europe led to the *Hungarian Uprising* (1956).

- Encouraged by *Khrushchev's* condemnation of *Stalin*, Nagy embarked his country on a 'new course' that led to less strict control of *communism* and greater economic and personal freedoms.
- Communist hard-liners hit back at Nagy and he lost power in 1955.
- Popular demonstrations in support of Nagy led to a full-scale revolt against the Russians. Nagy was returned to power and negotiated the departure of Russian tanks and troops from Hungary.
- Nagy's announcement that Hungary was going to withdraw from the *Warsaw Pact* to become a neutral state with allegiance to neither East nor West was unacceptable to Moscow. Russian troops returned in massive force and crushed the uprising. Nagy was captured, tried and executed.

TIP Nagy is a good example of an East European leader who learned at great cost that greater independence would only be achieved through successful armed revolt against the *Soviet Union*.

DS **Nasser, Gamal Abdul:** Egyptian president (1952–70).

- Nasser's domestic policies were dominated by a series of social and economic reforms to provide his people with better living standards. He oversaw the building of the Aswan dam on the River Nile to provide Egyptian farmers with irrigation.
- Nasser nationalised the Suez Canal in 1956, an act which led to the *Suez Crisis*.
- Nasser's *foreign policy* rested on *neutrality* in the *Cold War* (1945–91) and conflict with Israel during the second and third *Arab–Israeli Wars*. His aim of uniting all the Arab peoples in an Arab Union met with limited success.

TIP Nasser was important in the pan-Arabic movement to reduce Western interests and influence in the Middle East.

National Government: the *coalition governments* formed in Britain (1931–35 and 1935–45) to help unify the country during times of crisis.

- The *Depression* was the major crisis facing the country in 1931. Prime Minister *MacDonald* formed a National Government after the *Labour* government split over cuts in unemployment benefit. His decision to invite representatives from the *Conservative* and *Liberal* parties cost MacDonald his party membership.
- The National Government won a landslide victory in the 1935 general election. In reality, however, it was dominated by Conservatives, as demonstrated by the fact that its next three leaders (*Baldwin, Chamberlain* and *Churchill*) were all Conservative MPs.
- In addition to tackling the problem of high unemployment throughout the 1930s, the National Government was in power during the *Second World War* (1939–45).

TIP National Government was an important feature of British political history between 1931 and 1945.

DS **National Industrial Recovery Act (NIRA), 1933:** part of *Roosevelt's New Deal* to revive US industry.

- The act set up the National Recovery Administration (NRA) to control prices, limit production, establish codes for fair business competition and guarantee workers the right to set up a *trade union*.
- Big business interests opposed the act and many manufacturers and factory owners refused to abide by its codes.
- After hearing the *Sick Chicken Case* in 1935, the *Supreme Court* declared the federal government had exceeded its powers and that the NRA was illegal.

TIP NIRA was testimony to the New Deal belief in national planning and government action as opposed to a laissez-faire economy.

nationalisation: the taking over of the ownership of private property, industry or agriculture under the control of the state for common distribution.

- Typical measures include the state running of banks, hospitals, railways, iron and steel, and electricity.

TIP Nationalisation is a key feature of communist and socialist doctrine.

nationalism: the pursuit of strong common bonds of language, culture and history among people that is often expressed through devotion or loyalty to the mother country.

- Nationalist movements often seek the rights of *national self-determination* in order to make the nation strong, independent and united.

national self-determination: the principle that each nation has the right to exist, independent of foreign interference and free to govern its own affairs.

- The principle guided President *Wilson* at the *Paris Peace Conference* (1919–20).
- Following the *Great War* (1914–18), national self-determination was applied to

the creation of the Baltic States, but not to Austro-Hungarian relations, or the inclusion of Czechs, Slovaks, Hungarians, Ukrainians and Germans in the establishment of the new state of Czechoslovakia.

TIP National self-determination contributed to the collapse of the Austro-Hungarian and Ottoman empires in 1919.

DS **National Socialism:** the extreme political philosophy of the National Socialist Workers Party (Nazi Party) from 1920 to 1945.

- *Hitler* was an early member of the German Workers' Party; in 1920 the Nazi Party succeeded it and a year later he was declared sole leader.
- According to Nazi doctrine, the individual was a servant to the state, which in turn was a servant to the party ruled by Hitler.
- National Socialist doctrine was anti-republican, anti-communist, anti-democratic, anti-*Versailles* and *anti-Semitic*.
- Between 1933 and 1945, National Socialism was the ideology of the entire German state under the dictatorship of Hitler. At the end of the *Second World War* (1939–45), National Socialism was banned and the Nazi Party disbanded.

TIP National Socialist ideology set the stage for the largest and most costly war the world has suffered.

nation state: a community, or nation, of people with mainly common language, history, and culture who inhabit an independent sovereign state.

NATO: see *North Atlantic Treaty Organisation.*

DS **Nazi:** see *National Socialism.*

Nazi–Soviet Pact, 1939: a non-aggression agreement between the *Soviet Union* and Germany that opened the way for the invasion and partition of Poland.

- Also known as the Molotov–Ribbentrop Pact or the Hitler–Stalin Pact, it was supposed to last for 10 years and included an undertaking of *neutrality* in case either country became involved in war.
- Secret clauses provided for the carving up of Poland, Finland, Lithuania, Latvia and Estonia.
- Hitler agreed to the pact to avoid the threat of war on two fronts (Britain and France in the West and the Soviet Union in the East), while Stalin wanted time to rebuild the *Red Army* (which had been decimated during the *Great Terror*) and also to provide a barrier against Hitler.

TIP The Nazi–Soviet Pact was a temporary marriage of convenience between two dictators. Not only did it make war with Poland inevitable, but it also ended any possibility of an East–West alliance that would effectively have surrounded Germany.

DS **NEP:** see *New Economic Policy.*

Neuilly, Treaty of, 1919: the peace agreement between Bulgaria and the Allies after the *Great War* (1914–18).

- Modelled on the Treaty of *Versailles* (1919), the treaty forced Bulgaria to *cede* some territories to Yugoslavia and Romania. Additionally, Greece was given control of western Thrace and the Bulgarian Army was limited to 20,000 men.
- Bulgaria was also charged with war responsibility and made liable for reparation payments.

TIP Fear that severe terms in the Balkans would lead only to new war in the region led to less harsh terms for Bulgaria than for other defeated powers.

neutrality: a policy of supporting neither of two opposing sides, especially in an international dispute or during a war.

DS **New Deal:** *Roosevelt's* social and economic reforms of 1933–39, to tackle conditions resulting from the *Depression.*

- The first New Deal (1933–35) aimed at relief and recovery from unemployment while the second New Deal (1935–39) was primarily concerned with employment rights and the social security of the working population.
- Roosevelt set up numerous agencies that regulated the US economy under government supervision.
- Many industrialists were opposed to the New Deal and in 1936 the government and the *Supreme Court* clashed over the issue of its constitutional legality.
- Partial economic recovery was achieved and Roosevelt was elected to an unprecedented third term in office. However, full recovery came only with US involvement in the *Second World War* (1939–45).

TIP The New Deal laid the foundation of the US welfare system and increased the responsibility of the federal government to offer relief to the jobless and the needy. At the same time, it failed in its fundamental purpose of putting people back to work. More than 10 million US citizens were still jobless in 1939.

DS **New Economic Policy (NEP), 1921–28:** a communist policy modification instituted by *Lenin* to replace *war communism.*

- Peasant riots and disturbances highlighted the failure of war communism to address poor agricultural productivity and food shortages.
- The *NEP* allowed some freedom of internal trade and private ownership of farms and small businesses.
- While it led to a modest economic recovery for the peasants, the NEP did not address the fundamental Bolshevik concern of peasant ownership of land in a communist state. *Stalin* and his *Five-Year Plans* resolved the matter ruthlessly.

TIP The failure of the New Economic Policy to spark any real recovery in heavy industry led to the Treaty of *Rapallo* (1922) with Germany.

DS **New Frontier:** President *Kennedy's* domestic programme for social justice.

- President Kennedy pledged federal aid to education, medical care for the elderly, government action to strengthen the economy and an end to racial discrimination.

- Kennedy faced powerful opposition from a *Congress* dominated by conservative Republicans and southern Democrats. Consequently, his early performance in the struggle for racial equality — the most important domestic issue of the time — left many civil rights supporters disappointed.

TIP The New Frontier promised more than it could deliver. Despite initial lack of support from Kennedy, civil rights advocates made great and often painful strides through non-violent civil disobedience.

DS **Nicholas II:** tsar (emperor) of Russia (1894–1917) and the last member of the Romanov dynasty to rule the country.

- Nicholas II's German-born wife, Alexandra, was a strong believer in the tsarist tradition and influenced her husband heavily.
- Industrial unrest, bad harvests and defeat in the *Russo-Japanese War* (1905) led to the *Revolution of 1905*, which forced Nicholas to summon a *Duma*. Despite this he remained distrustful of representative government.
- Nicholas II's *foreign policy* was closely linked to the *Alliance system* (Russia became a close ally of France) which drew Russia into the *Great War* (1914–18).
- An almost unbroken string of disastrous military setbacks and the economic strains of war led to the *February Revolution* (1917). Nicholas was forced to abdicate and less than a year later the Bolsheviks murdered him and his family.

TIP Nicholas's character and policies — in particular his unwillingness or inability to be reconciled to the idea of genuine constitutional reform — were significant factors in creating the conditions for the revolutions that overthrew him.

DS **Night of the Long Knives, 1934:** the killing of several hundred of *Hitler's* enemies in the Nazi Party by the *SS*.

- Increased frustration among the *brownshirts* — who felt themselves to be neglected and unrewarded following the Nazi seizure of power — persuaded Hitler that the time had come to eliminate the leadership of the SA in order to prevent a 'second revolution'.
- Under the leadership of Roehm, the SA had become a powerful organisation regarded by its leadership as the true military force of Nazi Germany.
- This dismayed army generals, who were only too willing to support Hitler's purge of the party. At least 100 of his enemies were murdered, including Roehm.

TIP The Night of the Long Knives removed one of two remaining obstacles to the Nazi consolidation of power. When *Hindenburg* died a few weeks later, Hitler assumed the powers of president and gave himself the title Führer, or leader, which completed his mastery over Germany.

DS **NIRA:** see *National Industry Recovery Act.*

Nivelle Offensive, 1917: a failed French military offensive under General Nivelle's command that resulted in massive casualties and mutiny in the French army.

- The French expected to drive 6 miles into the German line on the first day of the attack. They managed 600 yards. General Nivelle persisted and after 2 weeks of slaughter French casualties stood at almost 200,000.
- Widespread mutiny resulted; it was reported at one stage that almost half the entire French army was refusing to obey orders.
- General Pétain replaced Nivelle. Pétain restored order by improving living conditions for thousands of French soldiers. He also tried and executed hundreds of the ringleaders of the mutiny to serve both as punishment and an example for others.

TIP

Nivelle was the last major French attack of the *Great War* (1914–18). So serious were the mutinies, that the French government warned its allies to expect no further French offensive action for some time.

DS **Nixon, Richard:** the US Republican president (1969–74) whose administration is mostly remembered for the *Watergate Affair* (1972–74).

- With the assistance of Henry *Kissinger*, Nixon produced a thaw in the *Cold War* (1945–91). He pursued *détente*, signed the SALT I Treaty (1972), became the first US president to visit China and travelled to Moscow for talks with *Brezhnev*.
- In 1969 he declared the Nixon Doctrine. This marked a shift in US *foreign policy* away from its many overseas commitments to a greater reliance on regional allies to combat world *communism*.
- In the face of rising domestic opposition to the *Vietnam War* (1946–75), Nixon oversaw the withdrawal of US forces from Southeast Asia.
- It was his illegal activities during the 1972 presidential campaign that forced Nixon to become the first US leader to resign.

TIP

Despite foreign policy successes, Nixon is mostly remembered as a corrupt and unscrupulous leader whose legacy was to leave the US people with the realisation that their government was rotten to the core.

DS **NKVD:** the People's Commissariat of Internal Affairs, or state security police, in the *Soviet Union* from 1934 to 1943.

- The NKVD was chiefly responsible for administering the *Gulag* camp system and serving as the main instrument of the *Great Terror*.

TIP

Without the NKVD, *Stalin* would not have been able to generate the climate of fear and terror that was so integral to his rule.

DS **no-man's land:** the area that separated enemy trenches during the *Great War* (1914–18).

- No-man's land was characterised by deep shell holes, barbed wire and dead soldiers.
- Any soldier who ventured into no-man's land during daylight hours almost invariably met death or serious injury.

TIP No-man's land is closely associated with stalemate and the futility of *trench warfare*. See also *Western Front*.

Non-Aggression Pact: see *Nazi–Soviet Pact*.

Normandy Landings: see *D-Day*.

North Atlantic Treaty Organisation (NATO): a military alliance formed by 12 Western European nations after the *Berlin Airlift* (1948–49) for purposes of mutual defence during the *Cold War* (1945–91).

- The US was the alliance's strongest member. Other founder countries were Britain, France, Belgium, Holland, Luxemburg, Portugal, Denmark, Ireland, Italy, Norway and Canada.
- Greece and Turkey joined NATO in 1952 and West Germany joined in 1955. France formally withdrew in 1955.
- Since the end of the Cold War in 1991, several ex-*Warsaw Pact* states such as Poland and Hungary have joined as a defence against the threat of Russian dominance.

TIP The North Atlantic Treaty Organisation and the Warsaw Pact were the two most important Cold War military alliances.

DS **NRA:** National Recovery Administration. See *National Industry Recovery Act*.

Nuclear Test Ban Treaty, 1963: an agreement between the *Soviet Union*, the US and Britain to stop all nuclear tests except underground ones.

- Since the 1950s, concern had been growing about the effects of radioactive fallout caused by above-ground nuclear testing.
- The treaty was a direct reaction to the *Cuban Missile Crisis* (1962) when the two superpowers came dangerously close to war. Neither *Khrushchev* nor *Kennedy* wanted to bring about a nuclear exchange.
- France and China were set to conduct tests of their own and refused to sign the Nuclear Test Ban Treaty. A year later, China detonated its first nuclear weapon.

TIP The Nuclear Test Ban Treaty is a good example of *détente* and the recognition by both superpowers of the risk of *mutually assured destruction* (MAD) resulting from any conflict that included the use of nuclear weapons.

nuclear warfare: a type of armed conflict involving the use of *atomic* and *hydrogen* bombs.

- The consequences of full nuclear war would be disastrous, to say the least. For this reason it has generally been thought that the existence of such weapons acts as a deterrent against their use.

DS **Nuremberg Laws, 1935:** a series of laws used to isolate German Jews in Nazi Germany.

- The discriminatory laws were made public at the 1935 Nazi Party rally and enforced from September of that year.

- There were two laws: the Reich Law of Citizenship deprived Jews of German citizenship and classed them as the 'subject of the state'; the Law for the Protection of German Blood and Honour forbade intermarrying between Jews and Gentiles and banned sexual relations outside marriage between the two groups.

TIP These laws became a rallying call for Nazi racial philosophy, emphasised the Nazi notion of racial purity, and set Germany on the path to the *Final Solution*.

DS **Nuremberg rallies:** Nazi propaganda in the form of extravagant political celebrations to drum up support for *Hitler* and German *nationalism*.

- Each year between 1923 and 1936 tens of thousands of Nazi supporters gathered to pay homage to Hitler. Each rally was grander than the previous one.

TIP The Nuremberg rallies were so well staged that hundreds of thousands of ordinary Germans were spellbound or brainwashed.

DS **Nuremberg Trials:** the international military tribunal held (1945–46) to try the major Nazi figures for crimes associated with the *Second World War* (1939–45).

- Nuremberg was chosen as the location of the trials mainly because it had been the site of the *Nuremberg rallies*. The judges and prosecutors were American, British, French and Russian.
- Twenty-one Nazis were put on trial for crimes against peace and humanity. Eleven were hanged while several others received prison sentences.

TIP The Nuremberg tribunal put the Third Reich itself on trial as well as its most notorious surviving members. The Nazi Party was declared an illegal organisation and outlawed, as were the *SS* and *Gestapo*.

DS **October Manifesto of 1905:** a proclamation of political reform made by *Nicholas II* following the *Revolution of 1905*.

- On *Witte's* advice, Nicholas accepted the creation of the *Duma* and promised to introduce civil liberties including freedom of speech, assembly and worship.
- While the manifesto placated middle-class liberals, it did nothing for the peasants or industrial workers.
- The peasants were bought off with government assurances. The workers were dealt with by suppression rather than concession and the government quickly crushed their strikes.

TIP Without the October Manifesto, Nicholas II would not have survived the 1905 revolution. The creation of the Duma led many people to believe Nicholas would share power with the middle class, or bourgeois. Their wait-and-see attitude to government reform deprived the revolutionaries of their single biggest power base.

DS **October Revolution of 1917:** the act that led to the Bolshevik seizure of power in Russia.

- Under the leadership of *Trotsky*, Bolshevik forces seized the *Provisional Government* (1917) in the Winter Palace.
- There was hardly any resistance to the Bolshevik takeover of several key points in *Petrograd*. Within a week, Moscow and other Russian cities had fallen under Bolshevik control.
- On 7 November 1917, the All-Russian Congress of Soviets recognised the authority of the Bolsheviks, who set up their own executive body. *Lenin* immediately promised the peasants 'peace, land and bread' and announced the end of Russian involvement in the *Great War* (1914–18).

TIP The events of the October Revolution have fuelled controversy surrounding the question of whether it was Trotsky rather than Lenin who was truly responsible for the Bolshevik seizure of power.

O

DS **OGPU:** the United State Political Administration, the state security police in the *Soviet Union* from 1923 to 1934.

- *Stalin* used OGPU to enforce *collectivisation* and to run political trials and the labour camp system.
- The *NKVD* replaced OGPU in 1934.

DS **oil crisis:** an international problem in the early 1970s when the oil-producing Arab states attempted to use oil as a weapon against those countries that actively supported Israel.

- In an effort to force the Israelis to restore Palestinian rights and withdraw from the land conquered in 1967, the Organisation of Petroleum Exporting Countries (OPEC) cut production and raised oil prices.
- The result was petrol shortages and queues of consumers at petrol stations throughout many West European countries and the US.
- The discovery of alternative sources of energy led to a drop in consumption of oil and a stabilising of oil prices that ended the crisis.

TIP

Since Israel did not get its oil from the Arab states, the political effect of the price rise was minimal and the use of oil as a weapon met with only limited success.

DS **Okhrana:** the secret police used by *Nicholas II* to control and arrest his political opponents.

- Political prisoners, including *Lenin*, were sent to labour camps in Siberia run by the Okhrana.

Overlord, Operation: see *D-Day*.

OVRA: *Mussolini's* secret police set up in 1927 to spy on anti-fascist individuals and groups in Italy.

Pact of Steel, 1939: an agreement between *Hitler* and *Mussolini* to bind Germany and Italy into a military alliance to end British and French hopes that a wedge could be driven between the two dictators.

- When Germany invaded Poland in September 1939, Mussolini had no intention of fighting a war. He did not actually honour the pact he made with Hitler until June 1940.
- Along with the *Nazi–Soviet Pact* (1939), the Pact of Steel reassured Hitler that he would not have to fight a two-front war.

TIP Mussolini's decision to draw his country militarily closer to Germany was influenced by the fact that Italy appeared an increasingly junior partner to growing German power and menace.

DS **Palestine:** the land along the east coast of the Mediterranean that is at the centre of the Arab struggle for independence, and the Jewish demand for a homeland.

- Palestine was part of the Ottoman Empire until the British conquered it in 1917. It became a British mandate in 1920.
- The *Balfour Declaration* (1917) and *Zionism* led to an influx of Jews to Palestine in the 1920s. This resulted in tension and violence.
- Following the *Holocaust*, Jewish immigration reached levels that placed great strain on the British authorities. Attempts to control the numbers of Jews arriving to settle in Palestine led to a campaign of terrorism by groups like *Irgun* and the *Stern Gang*.
- In 1947 the *United Nations* voted for the partition of Palestine into a Jewish state and an Arab state. A year later, *Ben Gurion* announced the birth of Israel. Since then, the division of land has been the cause of almost uninterrupted violent conflict between the Palestinians and the Israelis, despite numerous attempts at conciliation such as the *Camp David Agreement* (1978).

TIP The struggle for control of Palestine is one of the most divisive and bitter conflicts in modern history. It is still unresolved.

DS **Palestine Liberation Organisation (PLO):** an umbrella group for the main armed Palestinian movements, whose goal is to regain the land lost to Israel in 1948–49 and create an Arab–Palestinian state by both force and political pressure.

- The most notable group within the PLO is *Al Fatah,* which is led by *Arafat.*
- The PLO waged *guerrilla warfare* and *terrorism* against Israelis at home and abroad. Bombings, hijackings and the murder of Israeli athletes at the 1972 Olympics brought Palestinian demands to the attention of the world.
- Direct peace talks were held between Israel and the PLO in 1993. They led to peace deals guaranteeing the Palestinians limited self-rule in their own lands.

TIP Arafat's recent moderation of the PLO has led to the rise of more extreme Palestinian groups such as Hamas.

DS **Pankhurst, Emmeline:** the leader of the British *suffragette* movement who believed that governments would improve social conditions only when sufficient pressure was put on them by women achieving the right to vote.

- Pankhurst founded the Women's Political and Social Union. Her frustration at the lack of equality led her to resort to violent tactics for which she served time in prison.
- During the *Great War* (1914–18), she encouraged women to support the war effort by going into industry and the armed services.

TIP Pankhurst is a key figure in the struggle for women's rights and the vote in Britain.

Panmunjon: a Korean village in the demilitarised zone separating North and South Korean forces where the *armistice* to halt the *Korean War* (1950–53) was signed.

- Although peace talks began in 1951, two more years passed before the armistice.
- The North Koreans were forced to modify a hard-line position following the death of *Stalin,* who had been a staunch supporter and ally of *Kim Il Sung.*
- In addition to the repatriation of prisoners of war, the North–South Korean borderline was set near the Thirty-Eighth Parallel, the prewar boundary.

TIP Panmunjon did not lead to a formal peace treaty between North and South Korea, meaning that technically the two sides remain locked in a state of war.

Paris Peace Conference, 1919–20: a gathering of former enemies in the *Great War* (1914–18) formally to end the conflict and determine the postwar peace settlement.

- The Treaty of *Versailles* between Germany and the Allies was the main treaty that resulted. It was signed in 1919.
- The Treaty of *Saint-Germain* (1920) dealt with Austria, the Treaty of *Neuilly* (1919) with Bulgaria, the Treaty of *Trianon* (1919) with Hungary, and the Treaty of *Sevres* (1920) dealt with the Ottoman (Turkish) Empire.

TIP

The treaties drawn up at Paris remained controversial to those who felt they were too harsh and those who complained they did not go far enough in punishing the defeated powers. This was a significant factor contributing to the breakdown of international order and stability in the 1930s.

Paris Peace Talks, 1968–73: the search for a peaceful solution to the *Vietnam War* (1946–75) that resulted in a cease-fire and the eventual withdrawal of US troops.

- Faced with serious opposition to the war within his own country and troubled by the rising cost of US involvement, *Johnson* stopped the bombing of North Vietnam and asked Hanoi to begin negotiations.
- Peace talks dragged on for 5 years before a cease-fire was agreed.
- Southern Vietnamese fears were allayed by US promises to defend the South if the North violated the agreement. However, both sides quickly broke the cease-fire and full-scale warfare erupted again, leading to the collapse of the Saigon government and victory for the North.

TIP

US intentions and actions should be studied in the context of the *Cold War* (1945–91), *détente*, and the *Sino-Soviet split*, all of which made a cease-fire easier for *Kissinger* to negotiate.

Paris Peace Treaties, 1947: an agreement between the Allies and Germany's allies (Italy, Hungary, Finland, Bulgaria and Romania) following the *Second World War* (1939–45).

- The main provisions were that Italy lost land to Yugoslavia, Trieste became a 'free city', and Finland and Romania lost territory to the *Soviet Union*. Hungary was returned to its pre-1939 borders.

peaceful coexistence: *Khrushchev's* idea that the socialist and capitalist systems could exist side by side.

- The notion of peaceful coexistence came from Khrushchev's view that nuclear weapons made war between the two superpowers unthinkable.
- This led to an easing of *Cold War* (1945–91) tension and Khrushchev's suggestion that Moscow would tolerate different brands of *communism*.

TIP

Peaceful coexistence was not a sign of Khrushchev's lack of commitment to communism. He wanted the downfall of capitalism, but felt this would come about not through conflict but by capitalism collapsing of its own accord.

DS **Pearl Harbor, 1941:** Japanese carrier-borne aircraft attacked the main US naval base in Hawaii on 7 December, without a formal declaration of war.

- In less than 2 hours, 19 ships were sunk or disabled and some 2,400 people killed. *Congress* declared war on Japan the day after the attack.

TIP

On 11 December, Germany and Italy honoured the *Tripartite Pact* (1940) with Japan and declared war on the US.

p

DS **perestroika:** *Gorbachev's* reform programme to modernise the highly bureaucratised and decaying Soviet economy.
- *Perestroika* was introduced in 1985 but had a limited impact on economic performance and could not prevent the collapse of the USSR 6 years later.

TIP Along with *glasnost*, *perestroika* formed the basis of Gorbachev's domestic policies.

DS **permanent world revolution:** the belief among some Russian communists that efforts to bring about revolutions in the wider world were a greater priority than attempts to modernise Russia.
- The doctrine of permanent world revolution was closely associated with *Trotsky* and his supporters in the 1920s. They argued that only a world *proletariat* revolution could solve 'the contradictions in the position of a workers' government in a backward country with an overwhelmingly peasant population'.
- Permanent world revolution was counter to *Stalin's* belief in the doctrine of *socialism in one country*, which looked first and foremost to the construction of a 'complete socialist society' in the USSR.

TIP The two competing doctrines defined the ideological ground during the struggle between Trotsky and Stalin to succeed *Lenin* as leader.

DS **Petrograd:** the name for the Russian city of St Petersburg from 1914 to 1924.
- St Petersburg's name was changed at the beginning of the *Great War* (1914–18) because it sounded too German.
- Following *Lenin's* death in 1924, the city was renamed Leningrad in honour of the late Bolshevik leader.
- It was once again named St Petersburg following the collapse of communist rule in the 1990s.

DS **Phoenix Program:** secret US attempts to capture or kill *Vietcong* leaders in the South during the *Vietnam War* (1946–75).
- Phoenix was organised by the *Central Intelligence Agency* and introduced in 1967.
- Some 60,000 people were killed during its operation (1967–73).
- When the existence of the programme became public knowledge in the US, it resulted in heavy criticism of US policy and undermined support for the war.

TIP Along with a significant increase in US combat troops and intensified bombing of North Vietnam, the Phoenix Program was part of US escalation of the conflict and an attempt to halt the flow of arms and men from the North to their fighters in the South.

Phoney War: term used to describe the first several months of land warfare in Europe during the *Second World War* (1939–45).
- Between September 1939 and May 1940 there was little combat, except in Poland.

- Several costly British air raids on German industry and military sites were the major highlight of the fighting.
- The first British army death due to enemy action was near the end of December 1939.
- Both sides used this period to wage a propaganda war and to build up military preparedness.

TIP The Phoney War came to an end in May 1940 when Hitler sent forces into Holland, Belgium and France.

plebiscite: a vote on a single issue taken by all the people in a particular area.
- According to the Treaty of *Versailles* (1919), a plebsicite was to be held in the *Saar* area to allow the people of the region to decide whether to live under *League of Nations* (1920–45) control, to return to Germany, or to become part of France.
- When 90% of the Saar electorate voted to become part of Germany again, large resources of coal, iron and steel went with them.

TIP The Saar plebiscite was the first step towards *Hitler's* goal of uniting the German-speaking peoples and he used the vote as evidence of popular support for his government.

DS **PLO:** see *Palestine Liberation Organisation.*

pogrom: from the Russian word for 'destroy', it refers to a government-organised and backed massacre of a racial minority group.
- *Anti-Semitic* pogroms in Russia at the turn of the twentieth century forced thousands of Jews to emigrate to the West.
- Another example of a pogrom was *Kristallnacht* (1938).

Polish Corridor: the area of land between the Baltic Sea and the centre of landlocked Poland, established by the Treaty of *Versailles* (1919).
- Although the majority of the people living in the Polish Corridor were German, the Treaty of Versailles made Danzig a 'free city' to allow Poland access to the sea.
- *Hitler* demanded unrestricted access across the corridor to East Prussia. Poland's refusal to give in to his bullying was an immediate cause of the German invasion in September 1939.

TIP Hitler's attitude convinced *Chamberlain* that stronger measures were needed to prevent further German aggression and he persuaded the British and French governments to guarantee to protect Poland against any threat to its independence.

DS **Politburo:** the political bureau of the central committee of the Communist Party, a small group of leaders who governed policy making in the *Soviet Union.*
- The Politburo was set up by *Lenin* in 1917 to supervise the Communist Party of the Soviet Union when its Central Committee was not in session.
- It had final say in policy making and its decisions were irrevocable. *Stalin* used it to rubber stamp his views and policies.

Potsdam Conference, 1945: a meeting of the *Second World War* (1939–45) Allies (Britain, USSR, USA) following Germany's defeat.

- The *Yalta* decisions were confirmed and the USSR agreed to join the war against Japan, but there remained a gulf between the Russians and the two Western powers over *reparations* and the future of Poland.
- Britain was represented first by *Churchill* and then *Attlee* after the *Labour Party* won the 1945 general election. *Truman* replaced *Roosevelt* when the latter died before the conference.

TIP The new Western leaders took a strong dislike to *Stalin* and left the meeting convinced that force was the only thing the Russians would understand. This, and Truman's refusal to share atomic secrets with Stalin, led to the onset of the *Cold War* (1945–91).

Powers, Francis Gary: the US CIA pilot who was shot down and captured in 1960 by the Russians while flying a U-2 spy mission 1,200 miles inside the *USSR*.

- The U-2 was a high-flying and fast-moving plane that carried telescopic cameras.
- In mid-1960, *Cold War* (1945–91) tension was running high over Berlin and Germany. A summit meeting between *Khrushchev* and *Eisenhower* was set for Paris in May.
- Two weeks before the summit was due to start, Powers was captured and put on display along with the wreckage of his aircraft. Moscow demanded a public apology from Eisenhower for the incident. When Eisenhower refused to apologise, the Soviet delegation walked out of the Paris summit in protest. Powers was later handed over to the USA as part of a spy exchange.

TIP US government documents released at the end of the Cold War revealed that there had been thousands of US spy flights over the Soviet Union.

PR: see *proportional representation.*

Prague Spring, 1968: see *Dubcek.*

DS **Prohibition:** the banning of the manufacture, sale and transportation of alcoholic beverages by the US government in 1919.

- Prohibition was the climax of a long-running campaign against drunkenness and alcoholism. At first, the so-called 'noble experiment' caused per capita consumption of alcohol to drop.
- After 1925, Prohibition was widely ignored in US cities and criminal organisations responded to a public demand for alcohol.
- President *Roosevelt* ended Prohibition in 1933.

TIP See also *bootleggers.*

proletariat: *Marx's* term to describe the industrial working class, who worked in poor conditions for low wages.

- Marx believed the proletariat would rebel against their bosses and seize control of land, factories and mines. This is the essence of *communism.*

- Marx maintained that the proletarian revolution would occur in the industrial countries of Western Europe, not in Russia where the industrial class was very small. However, the first Marxist revolution took place in Russia in 1917.

TIP The struggle between the proletariat and the bourgeoisie are key concepts in the theory of communism.

proportional representation (PR): a system of voting to produce an election result in which membership of the elected assembly reflects the way the votes were cast.

- Under PR, a party that wins 10% of the votes cast would have 10% of the parliamentary representatives.

TIP The main criticism of PR is that it encourages a large number of political parties to be formed and that this leads to ineffective *coalition government*.

DS **Provisional Government, 1917:** the liberal regime that governed Russia in the period between the abdication of *Nicholas II* in March 1917 and the Bolshevik revolution 7 months later.

- The Provisional Government — first headed by Prince Lvov and then by *Kerensky* — favoured continuation of the war against Germany and the establishment of a *republic* in Russia.
- In *Petrograd*, the Bolshevik-controlled *soviet* issued its Order Number 1 commanding all Russian soldiers to disregard the Provisional Government and to obey soviet-issued orders instead.

TIP An understanding of Provisional Government weaknesses helps explain how the Bolsheviks came to power.

DS **Public Works Administration (PWA), 1933:** a US government agency established under the *National Industrial Recovery Act* with a brief to spur economic recovery.

- The PWA had $3.3 billion to hire the unemployed to build roads, sewage and water systems, public buildings and other government-run projects.
- The *Supreme Court* declared it unconstitutional in 1935.

TIP The Public Works Administration was a component of the *New Deal* and should be studied together with the *National Recovery Administration*.

purge: to murder government opponents indiscriminately, whether from the ranks of former government members, or from the military, or the population at large.

- *Stalin's* purges resulted in the mass expulsion of Communist Party members and the imprisonment, exile and execution of millions of Russian citizens.
- The *Night of the Long Knives* (1934) is another example of a political purge.

DS **putsch:** the German word describing a forcible takeover of a government.

- The term is closely associated with the *Kapp Putsch* in Berlin (1920) and the *Beer Hall Putsch* in Munich (1923).

Quebec Conference, 1944: a meeting between *Roosevelt* and *Churchill* to decide the political make-up of postwar Germany.

- Roosevelt and Churchill agreed that four occupation zones would be created, each controlled by one of the wartime allies (USSR, Britain, France, US). Both Germany and Austria were to be governed by an Allied Control Commission.

racism: the belief that one or more races are superior to others on the basis of physical or cultural differences.

- Racism can involve aggressive behaviour towards another race.
- The two most infamous examples of state-enforced racism in the twentieth century are South Africa (*apartheid*) and Nazi Germany (*anti-Semitism*).

Rapallo, Treaty of, 1922: an agreement by Germany and the *Soviet Union* to re-establish diplomatic relations.

- Germany and the Soviet Union also agreed to renounce financial claims on each other resulting from the *Great War* (1914–18), and pledged to cooperate on economic matters.

TIP Rapallo signified that both states had recovered from the diplomatic isolation caused by their respective defeats and revolutions.

DS **Rasputin, Grigorii:** a Russian priest who was an influential figure in Tsar *Nicholas II's* court.

- Rasputin gained his power from his ability to heal Nicholas and Alexandria's son and heir, Alexis.
- Rasputin's closeness to Alexandria encouraged him to interfere in politics and he became her chief adviser.
- His excessive personal behaviour and the suspicion among the Tsar's court that he was a German spy led to his murder in 1916.

TIP Rasputin played a key role in discrediting the Russian monarchy and undermining popular support for Nicholas.

DS **Reagan, Ronald:** US Republican president (1981–89).

- Reagan's economic measures were known as Reaganomics and involved cutting domestic expenditure and taxes. The result was a widening gap between rich and poor Americans.
- Reagan increased government spending on the US military and by 1985 defence spending accounted for more than one-third of the federal government's budget. This included the *Strategic Defence Initiative*.

- His anti-communist views guided US *foreign policy*. The Reagan Doctrine led to open and covert US intervention in civil wars in several less economically developed countries including Grenada and Nicaragua.
- A more moderate outlook during Reagan's second term led to a constructive relationship with *Gorbachev* and the *Intermediate Nuclear Forces Treaty* as well as *Strategic Arms Limitation Treaties.*
- In 1986 the Iran–Contra scandal broke when officials in Reagan's government were accused of selling arms to Iran in return for the release of US hostages held in Lebanon.

TIP The Reagan presidency witnessed a shift to the right in US politics as well as the collapse of the *Soviet Union* and the end of the *Cold War* (1945–91).

DS **Reconstruction Finance Corporation (RFC), 1932:** established by *Hoover* to make loans totalling $2 billion to banks, insurance companies and railways to help counter the effects of the *Depression*.

- The idea behind the RFC was to make loans to businesses at the top of the economic system in the hope of benefits filtering down to people at the bottom.
- Hoover was wedded to the political principle of hands-off government and the RFC was the most radical federal measure that his administration passed.

TIP The failure of the RFC fully to address the economic problems facing the US prepared the way for more direct federal intervention under the *New Deal.*

DS **Red Army:** the *Soviet Union* army set up by *Trotsky*.

- The Red Army was initially made up of workers and peasants to fight the *White Russians* during the Russian Civil War (1918–21).

DS **Red Scare, 1919:** anti-communist hysteria in the US, 1917–20.

- The Red Scare was caused by the *October Revolution of 1917* in Russia and fear that the US was about to be taken over by communists.
- Strikes and unrest in the steel industry were violently suppressed by management, who hired strikebreakers and depicted strike leaders as Bolsheviks.
- The Palmer Raids (1920) — in which federal agents throughout the US broke into meeting halls and homes without search warrants — disregarded elementary civil liberties.

TIP The Red Scare encouraged those who wanted tougher immigration laws. The federal response made it appear that *Wilson's* low tolerance of political dissent bordered on a fundamental distrust of democracy.

DS **Reichstag:** the building that housed the German parliament from 1871 to 1945.

- Before 1914, only men aged over 25 had the vote and the Reichstag merely approved laws passed by the king. It could not propose laws of its own and had little real power.
- Under the *Weimar* constitution, Germany was to be a democracy where men and women had the vote under a *proportional representation* electoral system.

TIP Between 1933 and 1945, the Reichstag was a Nazi-dominated assembly to rubber stamp *Hitler's* policies.

DS **Reichstag Fire, 1933:** the destruction of the *Reichstag* and an event that enabled *Hitler* to rush through laws establishing his position as German *dictator*.

- The Nazi government claimed the Reichstag fire was the first move in a communist conspiracy to seize power.
- The day after the fire, the Emergency Decrees for the Defence of Nation and State suspended civil liberties.

TIP When the decrees entered the constitution in March 1933, they abolished the rule of law and proclaimed a permanent state of emergency with Germany a police state under Hitler's control.

DS ***Rentenmark*:** the currency introduced in Germany in response to *hyperinflation*.

- *Stresemann* introduced the new currency when he became German chancellor in 1923.
- Stresemann used the *Rentenmark* to make it clear the government would not continue circulating a currency that was worth less than the paper it was printed on. His policy helped to renew consumer confidence.

TIP Knowledge of the *Rentenmark* helps explain both the causes of hyperinflation and Stresemann's attempts to spark a German economic recovery.

reparations: compensation made after a war to the victors by the defeated powers to help pay for the costs of the conflict.

- As part of the Treaty of *Versailles* (1919), Germany was required to pay £6,600 million in reparations to the Allies.
- This demand on the infant *Weimar Republic* became a major issue in Germany. The German people bitterly resented Article 231 of the Treaty of Versailles, which forced them to accept responsibility for causing the *Great War* (1914–18).
- German inability to pay reparations heightened international tension — especially between Germany and France — and eventually led to the *Dawes Plan* (1924) and the *Young Plan* (1929).
- In 1931 Germany ceased repayments and 2 years later an international conference agreed to give up all further reparations claims.

TIP The reparations issue is closely linked to *hyperinflation* (1923), the Belgo-Franco occupation of the *Ruhr* (1923–24), and the *Beer Hall Putsch* (1923). All four events should be studied closely together.

DS **Representation of the People Act, 1918:** the law that gave the vote to British men at the age of 21 and to women at the age of 30.

- The act was part of wider electoral reforms that came near the end of the *Great War* (1914–18) and highlighted the significant social, economic and political changes caused by the war.

- *Lloyd George* wanted voting rights for all men who had fought in the trenches and for women who had made a strong contribution to the war effort.
- Additionally, women were allowed to sit in the House of Commons and voting at general elections was to take place on the same day instead of being spread over several weeks.

TIP The Representation of the People Act should be studied alongside the women's suffrage movement, as the two are closely linked.

republic: a country that has a president or committee, rather than a monarch, as head of state and in which power rests in the hands of the people through their elected representatives.

- The *Weimar* (1919–33) and the US are two examples of twentieth-century republics.

DS **Republican Party:** one of the two main political US parties.

- The US Republican Party tends to be more conservative than the *Democratic Party*. It is often described as 'the party of big business' because its strength is drawn from the higher-income and professional classes.
- At home, Republicans favour less government spending, tax cuts, private enterprise and protectionism in trade.
- *Isolationism* tends to guide Republican *foreign policy*. This was temporarily abandoned between 1941 and 1945. Since then, Republican presidents have regarded Asia as a more important US interest than Europe.

revolution: a sudden, far-reaching change in a country's government that is often accompanied by violence.

- In a revolution, the political and social order is overturned and replaced by another.
- Revolutions typically involve large numbers of people as direct participants.

DS **Revolution of 1905:** violent opposition to Tsar *Nicholas II* that almost brought down his government.

- Its causes were defeat in the *Russo-Japanese War* (1904–05), the poor living conditions of the peasants and factory workers and the tsar's refusal to establish constitutional government.
- When government troops killed dozens of workers marching to present a petition to the tsar, revolution erupted. Workers' strikes were quickly followed by peasant riots and mutiny in the Black Sea Fleet.
- Nicholas survived because the army refused to join the revolutionaries, who were further split when the *October Manifesto* (1905) set up the *Duma*, or national parliament.

TIP The revolution revealed Nicholas II's unpopularity and his tenuous grip on power. He only addressed the grievances of his people superficially, and the 1905 revolution became a model for what later happened in 1917.

DS **RFC:** see *Reconstruction Finance Corporation*.

Rhineland, remilitarisation of, 1936: *Hitler's* first reversal of a major provision of the treaties of *Versailles* (1919) and *Locarno* (1925).

- Versailles forbade Germany to station troops on German territory west of the Rhine and on a 30-mile strip east of the river.
- Hitler sent in his army, with orders to withdraw if French troops moved to oppose the occupation. The absence of French or British resistance to the remilitarisation was part of a wider policy of *appeasement*.

TIP

Rhineland remilitarisation greatly increased Hitler's popularity in Germany and boosted his confidence in *foreign policy* matters; within 2 years, he had secured the *Anschluss* (1938) and annexed the *Sudetenland* (1938).

Rolling Thunder, Operation, 1965–68: the US Air Force bombing of North Vietnam.

- The air raids were part of an escalation of US involvement in the *Vietnam War* (1946–75) and came after *Johnson* proposed the *Tonkin Gulf Resolution* (1964) giving him authority to commit US ground troops to the conflict.
- The US air campaign was supposed to last 8 weeks but went on for three-and-a-half years. Its goals were to close North Vietnamese supply routes to the South and to convince the North to agree to a political compromise. Neither objective was achieved.

TIP

Some 3,500 US troops were sent to Vietnam in early 1965 to protect the air bases being used to bomb North Vietnam. By the end of the same year the number of US ground troops exceeded 200,000.

Rome, Treaty of, 1957: an agreement by six European countries to set up the European Economic Community (EEC).

- The original six member states were West Germany, France, Belgium, Holland, Italy and Luxembourg. All wanted closer European cooperation on economic matters.
- Signatory governments agreed to abolish tariff barriers between member states by 1967 and to allow free movement of capital, goods and labour.
- The treaty marked the first step towards closer European political and economic cooperation.

Rome–Berlin Axis, 1936: an agreement by *Hitler* and *Mussolini* to work together on matters of common interest.

- Mussolini had been drawn closer to the German dictator after the victory of his army in the *Abyssinian War* (1935–36) and the *League of Nations'* decision to impose economic *sanctions* on Italy.
- The Rome–Berlin Axis was followed by more formal agreements in the *Anti-Comintern Pact* (1937) with Japan and the *Pact of Steel* in 1939.

TIP

The Axis marked a significant reversal of Italian *foreign policy*, being signed a year after Mussolini agreed to the *Stresa Front* (1935) with Britain and France.

r

DS **Roosevelt, Franklin Delano (FDR):** the Democratic US president (1933–45) who led his country through the *Depression* and to victory in the *Second World War* (1939–45).

- Roosevelt's government was largely concerned with the *New Deal* and his promise of 'direct, vigorous action' to tackle the economic crisis.
- While the New Deal failed to put the US fully back to work, it renewed people's hope in their government and political leadership.
- Roosevelt's *foreign policy* steered away from the *isolationism* of the *Republican Party*. He helped Britain in its fight against *Hitler* and was instrumental in the passage of *lend–lease* aid.
- Roosevelt met *Churchill* and *Stalin* at the *Yalta Conference* (1945) to discuss the war against Germany.

TIP FDR died in 1945 at the start of his fourth term in office. Achieving four presidential election victories (in 1932, 1936, 1940 and 1944) is unsurpassed in US political history.

Ruhr: a German manufacturing region occupied by Belgian and French troops in 1923.

- The Ruhr occupation was a response to the Germans' failure to pay war *reparations*.
- The British and US governments condemned France and Belgium's action.
- The occupation met with passive resistance from German workers.
- Franco-German relations improved following the Treaty of *Locarno* (1925) and resulted in a French withdrawal from the Ruhr.

TIP The occupation brought little real benefit to the French but further undermined the *Weimar Republic* and contributed to the *Beer Hall Putsch* (1923).

Russo-Japanese War, 1904–05: a conflict caused by competing Russian and Japanese expansionism in the Far East and Manchuria, northern China and Korea.

- The war began with a surprise Japanese attack on the Russian fleet at *Port Arthur*, which was quickly followed by a series of defeats for the Russian army in Manchuria.
- The naval battle of Tsushima (1905) ended in a disastrous defeat for the Russians.
- The US-mediated Treaty of Portsmouth (1905) gave the Japanese control over Korea.

TIP The Russian defeat was a major factor in causing the *Revolution of 1905*.

DS **SA:** see *brownshirts.*

Saar: a German region rich in coal deposits.

- The *League of Nations* (1920–45) administered the Saar from 1919 until a *plebiscite* restored it to Germany in 1935.
- The overwhelming vote in favour of a return to German rule proved to *Hitler* that his government and policies had much popular support.

DS **Sacco and Vanzetti Case:** a US court case of the 1920s that highlighted the fear of radicalism in the US.

- Sacco and Vanzetti were two immigrant anarchists accused of involvement in robbery and murder. Though the evidence against them was flimsy, they were sentenced to death by a judge who openly sided with the prosecution.

TIP The Sacco and Vanzetti Case, the *Red Scare* (1919) and the Palmer Raids (1920) all fuelled anti-foreigner feelings in the USA in the 1920s.

DS **Sadat, Anwar:** president of Egypt (1970–81).

- Sadat succeeded *Nasser* and is best remembered for taking part in the *Camp David Agreement* (1978) and signing the Egypt–Israel Peace Treaty in 1979.
- Determined to recover the Sinai — the land east of the Suez Canal that Egypt lost in 1967 — Sadat launched the third *Arab–Israeli War* (Yom Kippur) in 1973.
- Although the war ended in an Israeli victory, Sadat emerged as a hero. He had broken the stalemate that existed before 1973 and forced the US to become more friendly with the Arab states.
- Sadat's popularity fell drastically after he made peace with Israel, an act that outraged many throughout the Arab world. Muslim fundamentalists assassinated him in 1981.

TIP Sadat was a key figure in the Middle East peace process.

Saint-Germain, Treaty of, 1919: the peace treaty between the Allies and Austria following the *Great War* (1914–18).

- Austria lost territory and, overall the Austrian population was reduced form its pre-1914 high of 28 million to 8 million.

- In addition, the *Anschluss* was forbidden, the Austrian army was limited to 30,000 men and Austria was made liable for *reparations* payments.

TIP

The harshness of this treaty was a factor explaining Austrian support for *Hitler* after he came to power in Germany.

SALT: see *Strategic Arms Limitation Treaties.*

sanctions: a form of punitive and coercive action — typically, an economic boycott — taken by one or more states against another.

- The most common economic sanction is a ban on trade.
- The goal is to weaken a state guilty of breaking international law enough to force it to back down.

TIP

Sanctions are difficult to enforce and are, therefore, rarely as effective as hoped. Twentieth-century examples of sanctions include those against Italy during its *Abyssinian War* (1935–36) and those imposed on the white government of South Africa in order to end *apartheid.*

Sarajevo: the capital of Bosnia where *Franz Ferdinand* was assassinated in 1914.

- In the 1990s, Serbs and Croats besieged Sarajevo during the Bosnian civil war.
- Today it is capital of Bosnia–Herzegovina.

TIP

Sarajevo was at the centre of ethnic conflict and the struggle for *national self-determination* at the beginning and end of the twentieth century.

satellite: a country that is under the political, military or economic control of a more powerful state.

- The term is most commonly used to describe the *Iron Curtain* countries under Moscow's dominance during the *Cold War* (1945–91).

Schlieffen Plan: the basis of the German attack that began the *Great War* (1914–18).

- The Schlieffen Plan was designed in 1905, and was based on the belief that any future war would be fought against France and Russia, probably supported by Britain.
- It called for a defensive war against Russia, while the French were to be swiftly defeated.
- A speedy advance was essential to the German plan of outflanking France by attacking through Belgium. It very nearly succeeded; but the Germans were halted outside Paris in the first Battle of the *Marne* (1914).

TIP

The Schlieffen Plan failed to take into account the military strength of the Russians, the power of Belgian resistance, the ability of the French to rush re-inforcements to the fighting, and the effectiveness of the *British Expeditionary Force.*

Schuschnigg, Kurt: the Austrian leader at the time of the *Anschluss* (1938).

- Schuschnigg became chancellor after Austrian Nazis murdered *Dolfuss* in 1934.

- Although not a strong supporter of democracy, Schuschnigg came to symbolise Austrian independence and resistance to Hitler's plan to unite Austria with Germany.
- He survived the *Second World War* (1939–45) and became a US citizen in 1956.

SDI: see *Strategic Defence Initiative.*

SEATO: see *South East Asia Treaty Organisation.*

Second World War, (1939–45): a worldwide conflict between the Axis powers (Germany, Italy and Japan) and the Allied powers (the British Commonwealth, the US and the *Soviet Union*) that left some 40 million people dead.

- The principal causes of the war were German resentment of the *Paris Peace Conference* (1919–20); the aggressive expansionist policies of Germany and Japan; British and French *appeasement* of *Hitler*; and US *isolationism.*
- The majority of the fighting took place in Europe and the Far East.
- Allied victory was followed by the *Cold War* (1945–91).

TIP The Second World War was the most devastating conflict in human history.

segregation: the separation of one group from the rest of the community, usually on racial or ethnic grounds.

- Segregation is a term closely associated with twentieth-century race relations in the US. See *desegregation.*
- In Nazi Germany, Jews and other so-called 'undesirables' were methodically and systematically segregated from the rest of the population.

Serbia: a Balkan state at the heart of the pre-1914 European movement for *national self-determination.*

- Although itself an independent state, Serbian policy before 1914 sought the liberation of Serb people within the Austro-Hungarian Empire.
- When a Serb nationalist assassinated *Franz Ferdinand* in the Bosnian capital of *Sarajevo,* it precipitated the *July Crisis* (1914) and the outbreak of the *Great War* (1914–18).
- After the break-up of Yugoslavia in the early 1990s, Serbia became embroiled in a civil war involving the two other former Yugoslav republics of Bosnia and Croatia.

Sevres, Treaty of, 1920: the peace treaty between Turkey and the Allies at the end of the *Great War* (1914–18).

- The Turks lost territory in the Middle East, which became *mandates* of the *League of Nations* (1920–45).
- Britain took control of Iraq and *Palestine.*
- The terms of the treaty caused enough resentment in Turkey to spark the revolution that put Mustafa *Kemal* in power.

TIP Kemal's refusal to accept the Treaty of Sevres led to the less harsh terms contained in the Treaty of *Lausanne* (1923).

DS **Sharpeville:** see *apartheid*.

DS **Sick Chicken Case, 1935:** a legal challenge that ended with the *Supreme Court's* decision to declare that the National Recovery Administration (NRA) was unconstitutional.

- A family-run poultry business challenged the NRA with formal objections to codes regulating prices, wages and competition.
- When the Schechter Poultry Corporation was found guilty of breaking a code by selling meat that was not fit for human consumption, it mounted a successful legal appeal in the Supreme Court.
- The court's decision to declare the poultry code illegal nullified 750 other NRA codes.

TIP The Sick Chicken Case effectively destroyed the NRA and seriously undermined the *New Deal*.

DS **Sinai:** a peninsula of northeast Egypt that has been the site of almost uninterrupted Arab–Israeli conflict since 1948.

- Israel seized a large part of the Sinai following the 1956 *Arab–Israeli War*.
- In the 1967, or Six-Day, War the Israelis occupied the whole of the peninsula.
- The *Camp David Agreement* (1978) and the subsequent peace treaty between Egypt and Israel saw the Israelis end their occupation and return the Sinai to Egypt in stages, but conflict over the region continues.

TIP Conflict over the Sinai contributed significantly to the enduring problem of the occupied territories.

Sino-Japanese War, 1937–45: a Far East conflict, sparked by Japanese expansionism which began with the invasion and occupation of *Manchuria*.

- Full-scale hostilities broke out in July 1937, following Japanese provocation of Chinese soldiers near Beijing.
- The major Chinese cities fell within weeks and the local populations subsequently fell victim to widespread Japanese abuse and atrocities.
- Chinese resistance came in the form of the *Guomindang* and the Chinese communists under Mao *Zedong*. During the *Second World War* (1939–45), the Chinese kept more than a million Japanese troops occupied on the mainland. In 1945 the Japanese surrendered to *Chiang*.

TIP The failure of the international community to react decisively to the Japanese invasion of China led the Japanese to act even more aggressively in the years to come.

Sino-Soviet split: a rift between China and the *Soviet Union* that first emerged in 1956.

- The two communist powers had always been uneasy allies, even more so after *Stalin* died in 1953.
- The Chinese were especially concerned by *Khrushchev's* attacks on his predecessor;

and worried that the Soviet Union no longer seemed interested in spreading communism.

- Further splits emerged over domestic, foreign and defence policies; in 1958, Khrushchev refused to give China any more help developing its nuclear arsenal.
- Sino-Soviet tension was highlighted 5 years later when the Chinese refused to join the US and the USSR in signing the *Nuclear Test Ban Treaty* (1963). China detonated its own *atomic bomb* in 1964.
- After a series of violent and bloody border clashes during the 1970s and 1980s, tension eased somewhat in the 1990s.

TIP The breakdown in Sino-Soviet relations encouraged China to be more open to the West and led to a warming of relations between China and Western powers.

DS **Six-Day War:** see *Arab–Israeli Wars.*

slump: see *Depression.*

Social Darwinism: a specious doctrine which maintains that certain races are more able and more intelligent than others.

- Social Darwinism is based on Darwin's theory of natural selection and the survival of the fittest.
- Several European powers used the doctrine to justify overseas expansion during the late nineteenth and early twentieth centuries. It was also an integral part of Nazi racial theories during the 1930s and 1940s.
- It is closely linked to the idea of eugenics, which held that selective breeding of humans could produce a perfect human race.

TIP Knowledge of Social Darwinism helps explain both European imperialism and the racial views of *Hitler.*

socialism: an economic and political ideology that advocates community (state) ownership and control of the means of production.

- Socialism is closely associated with the Marxist belief that whoever controls the means of production holds the power to determine how well people live.
- According to socialism, the needs of the community must come before the needs of the individual.
- Since the beginning of the twentieth century socialist movements have sprung up throughout the world.

TIP Marxist theory sees socialism as the transitional period in society's development from *capitalism* to *communism.*

DS **socialism in one country:** *Stalin's* slogan to gain support during his power struggle with *Trotsky* to succeed *Lenin* as ruler of the *Soviet Union.*

- Stalin believed *communism* should first be properly established in the Soviet Union and then exported via worldwide revolution. This ran counter to Trotsky's vision of *permanent world revolution.*
- Stalin successfully portrayed Trotsky's views as anti-Leninist and managed to

brand him as someone who lacked faith in the abilities of the Russian workers to construct a socialist state.

TIP 'Socialism in one country' and 'permanent world revolution' are slogans that summarised the power struggle between Stalin and Trotsky, and the former phrase is key to an understanding of Stalin's rise to power.

DS **Social Security Act, 1935:** an act that established several welfare programmes including a federal–state system of unemployment compensation, old age pensions and aid to dependent children in the USA.

- The Social Security Act was part of the *New Deal* and highlighted the federal government's acknowledgement of its responsibility to the aged, disabled people, the temporarily jobless and others in need of assistance.
- Certain employees (domestic servants, farm workers and many hospital and restaurant workers) were excluded from coverage.

TIP The act was a conservative measure in that workers and their bosses — rather than the government — paid for the benefits. Its significance is as a milestone on the road to direct federal government assistance for economically vulnerable American citizens.

Solidarity: a free and independent *trade union* in Poland that was the first of its kind in any East European communist country.

- Solidarity began in 1980 as a shipyard workers' protest against high prices and food and fuel shortages in a collapsing Polish economy.
- Lech Walesa, the leader of Solidarity, wanted the power to negotiate working conditions with the communist authorities.
- In 1982 the Polish government banned Solidarity and imprisoned its leaders. Though the move forestalled direct Soviet intervention in Polish affairs, it did not crush popular support for Solidarity.
- Following the collapse of *communism* in 1989, Poland became a democratic republic with Walesa as its first president.

TIP Solidarity became a powerful weapon used by President *Reagan* to undermine the *Iron Curtain*.

Somme, Battle of, 1916: the British and French offensive mounted to break the stalemate on the *Western Front* during the *Great War* (1914–18).

- First day (1 July) losses of 60,000 men set the costly tone for the entire offensive. Twenty weeks of bitter fighting saw the Allies advance a maximum of 10 miles and suffer 600,000 casualties.
- The Somme was the first battle to witness a deployment of tanks (by the British).

TIP Despite its apparent futility, the battle was a turning point in the war, as colossal German losses prevented it from again fielding a fully trained army of soldiers.

South East Asia Treaty Organisation (SEATO): an organisation
1954 to create an anti-communist barrier in Southeast Asia.

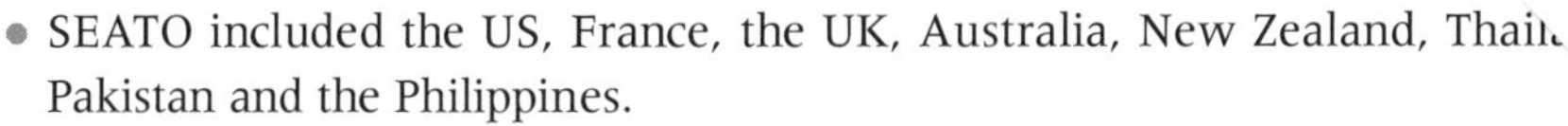

- SEATO included the US, France, the UK, Australia, New Zealand, Thail
Pakistan and the Philippines.
- The member states agreed to take joint action against aggression in a 'designated area'. Southern Vietnam, Laos and Cambodia were considered particularly vulnerable to the threat of communism.

TIP The fact that several member states never fully committed to the idea of *containment* in Southeast Asia led increasingly to direct US intervention in the *Vietnam War* (1946–75).

sovereignty: the source of political power of a state that is absolute and unlimited.

DS **soviet:** a local council of Russian workers, peasants and soldiers to represent the proletariat.

- Soviets were first formed during the *Revolution of 1905*.
- The model for further soviets was the St Petersburg Soviet (1905) led by *Trotsky*.
- At first the soviets worked democratically within the *Provisional Government* (1917). After a short while, however, the Bolsheviks took charge and used the soviets to spread a message of social and political reform.

TIP Bolshevik-dominated soviets played a key role in the success of the *October Revolution of 1917*.

DS **Soviet Union, 1923–90:** the communist-controlled union of 15 republics, each ruled by its own *soviet*; also known as the Union of Soviet Socialist Republics, or the USSR.

- In reality, important decisions affecting the Soviet Union were made by the *Politburo* in Moscow. The leaders of the Communist Party held most power.
- Ideological differences and mutual suspicion between the Soviet Union and the West led to the *Cold War* (1945–91).
- In 1991 the Soviet Union began to break up as several republics declared their independence from Moscow. *Yeltsin*, the president of the Russian Republic, then established the Commonwealth of Independent States as a loose replacement for the USSR.

TIP A good understanding of the history of the USSR is essential to explaining the Cold War and East–West relations throughout the twentieth century.

DS **Soweto:** a South African township at the heart of the struggle to end *apartheid*.

- Rioting erupted in Soweto in 1976 after the white government announced that all South African children were to be made to study Afrikaans, the language of the white minority.
- Police killed several hundred people before the government finally abandoned its plan to impose the language.

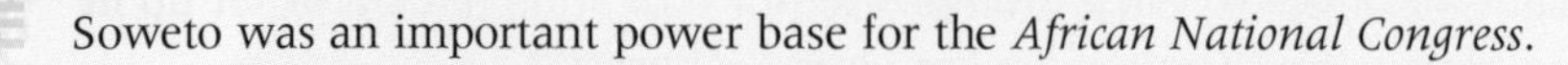

TIP Soweto was an important power base for the *African National Congress.*

Spanish Civil War, 1936–39: a conflict that followed a right-wing Nationalist rebellion to overthrow the elected republic.

- Nationalist forces were led by General *Franco* and included the Catholic church, landowners and a small fascist party.
- Socialists, liberals, communists, and other left-wing groups supported the government.
- Three years of fighting left 500,000 Spaniards dead.
- Several foreign governments took part to help the side whose ideas they supported. *Mussolini* and *Hitler* supported Franco, while the USSR backed the Republican side. Britain and France remained neutral, a decision that contributed to the Nationalist victory.

TIP The Spanish Civil War made the idea of war acceptable to many Europeans who saw the conflict as a prelude to the *Second World War* (1939–45).

DS **Spartacist Uprising, 1919:** an attempt by the German Communist Party to seize power from the *Weimar* government.

- The uprising was led by *Luxemburg* and *Liebknecht.* They sought to recreate in Germany what had taken place in Russia in 1917.
- *Ebert* used the *Freikorps* brutally to suppress the uprising. Both Liebknecht and Luxemburg were murdered.

TIP The failed uprising of 1919 — along with the *Kapp Putsch* (1920) and the *Beer Hall Putsch* (1923) — highlighted the political weakness and instability of the Weimar Republic during its infant years.

DS **speakeasies:** see *bootleggers.*

DS **SS (*Schutzstaffel*):** literally 'defence unit', the *Schutzstaffel* was formed under *Himmler's* leadership in 1925.

- *Hitler* used the SS to purge the SA during the *Night of the Long Knives* (1934).
- The SS grew to include armed (*Waffen*) groups, and ran concentration and *death camps* during the *Final Solution.*

TIP SS power within the *Third Reich* (1933–45) transformed it into a state within a state and an army within an army.

DS **Stakhanovite Movement:** an attempt to increase industrial output during the second *Five-Year Plan* in the *Soviet Union.*

- The movement was named after Alexis Stakhanov, a miner who exceeded his target by allegedly mining 102 tons of coal single-handed in the course of one overnight shift.
- Other workers were encouraged to copy the achievement and — officially, anyway — stood to gain higher wages and access to better housing and scarce consumer goods if they could match his reported efforts.

- Stakhanov's claim was shown to be false but was none the less the focus of government pressure for increased production.

TIP

Stalin used it for propaganda purposes to prove the power of *Bolshevism* to overcome any obstacle.

DS **Stalin, Joseph:** the Communist Party dictator of the *Soviet Union* from 1924 to 1953.

- Stalin rose through the ranks of the Bolsheviks after helping *Lenin* in the *October Revolution* (1905). In 1922 he became Secretary of the Communist Party, a position he held until his death.
- By 1928, Stalin had disposed of his rivals and introduced forced *collectivisation* and rapid industrialisation.
- To maintain absolute control, Stalin introduced the *Great Terror*. By 1941, millions of Soviet citizens had been charged with treason and condemned.
- As commissar of defence, Stalin led the USSR to victory in the *Second World War* (1939–45) and attended the conferences of the Allied leaders at *Tehran* (1943), *Yalta* (1945) and *Potsdam* (1945).
- After 1945, Stalin sought to retain tight control of the East European communist countries and to spread communism to Asia. He aided North Korea during the *Korean War* (1950–53).

Stalingrad: a city on the banks of the River Volga in southern Russia that was the scene of a decisive German defeat during the *Second World War* (1939–45).

- Stalingrad was a key objective in *Hitler's* plan to capture the Caucasus oilfields.
- Between August 1942 and January 1943, German and Russian forces fought bitterly throughout the city.
- Some 300,000 starving Germans were forced to surrender, making Stalingrad the biggest single German defeat of the war to date.

TIP

The battle for Stalingrad was the first time a Nazi army had been decisively defeated; Russian morale soared after the victory. This battle should be considered together with the Battle of *Kursk* (1943).

START: see *Strategic Arms Reduction Talks*.

Star Wars: see *Strategic Defence Initiative*.

DS **Stern Gang:** an armed Zionist group that fought British rule in *Palestine* 1940–48.

- Its founder, Abraham Stern, left *Irgun* when it suspended its anti-British campaign in Palestine during the *Second World War* (1939–45).
- The gang used various acts of *terrorism* against the British authorities and the Arab population. In 1948 it assassinated the *United Nations* mediator in the first *Arab–Israeli War*.
- It was dissolved in 1948, the year the birth of the state of Israel was declared.

TIP

The Stern Gang was the most violent of the Jewish groups fighting to establish a Zionist state.

DS **Stolypin, Peter:** Russian prime minister (1906–11).

- Stolypin introduced moderate land reform and restricted the right to vote in the *Duma*.
- He backed the *Kulaks* in the belief that they would support the government and not push for further political change.
- Stolypin also cracked down on revolutionaries and strikers and established special courts that condemned several thousand Russians to death.
- Stolypin was killed by a radical in 1911.

TIP Stolypin's reforms were a serious attempt to improve conditions in the Russian countryside. They were inspired by his goal of preserving the essentially conservative nature of Russian politics and society.

Strategic Arms Limitation Treaties (SALT), 1972 and 1979: negotiations between the US and the *Soviet Union* to limit the nuclear arms race during the *Cold War* (1945–91).

- The first treaty (1972) limited the building of middle-range weapons for 5 years. It did not, however, reduce existing stockpiles of nuclear weapons.
- In 1979 *Carter* and *Brezhnev* agreed on a second treaty limiting the number of long-range missiles, particularly those with multiple warheads.
- The Soviet invasion of *Afghanistan* (1979) brought SALT talks to a halt and the US *Congress* refused to ratify the agreement.

TIP The failure of the US and the Soviet Union to cap their diplomacy with a concrete agreement resulted in the end of *détente* and renewed *Cold War* (1945–91) hostility.

Strategic Arms Reduction Talks (START), 1991: a US–Russian agreement to destroy about one-third of their nuclear weapons.

- *Reagan* started negotiations in 1982. He wanted to reduce — and not just limit — nuclear weapons.
- While Reagan and the Soviet leader *Gorbachev* agreed in principle to an arms reduction, disagreement over the *Strategic Defence Initiative*, or Star Wars, blocked any formal treaty.
- By 1991, relations between the two powers had improved and the START-I Treaty was signed. It reduced each side's nuclear warheads to 6,000. A year later a second START treaty was agreed. It provided for the reduction of warheads to about 3,000 each side by 2003.

TIP The START treaties came at the time of the collapse of the *Soviet Union* and marked the final chapter in the *Cold War* (1945–91).

Strategic Defence Initiative (SDI): a US plan for an anti-missile defence system in space.

- *Reagan* announced SDI in 1983. It was nicknamed Star Wars after the science fiction film.

- SDI involved the development of anti-satellite lasers to destroy incoming nuclear missiles.
- The announcement of Star Wars research and development led to considerable tension between the US and the *Soviet Union* and a renewal of the *Cold War* (1945–91).

TIP

Even though the US was unable to develop the necessary technology, SDI remained controversial because, if realised, it would have signified a shift in the balance of power. It also suggested that the US government felt it could wage and win a nuclear war.

Stresa Front, 1935: a combined British, French and Italian attempt to block growing German militarisation.

- France, Britain and Italy condemned the reintroduction of conscription and rearmament in Germany. They also agreed to stand together against any German aggression.
- The front quickly fell apart, however, when Britain upset France by signing the *Anglo-German Naval Treaty* (1935) and after Italy started the *Abyssinian War* (1935–36).

TIP

The Stresa Front provided an early and real opportunity to halt German expansionism. The reasons behind its short life help explain how and why future attempts to do the same proved unsuccessful.

DS **Stresemann, Gustav:** German chancellor (1923) and foreign minister (1923–29).

- Stresemann was leader of the National Liberals, renamed the German People's Party in 1919.
- His greatest achievements were to end Germany's diplomatic isolation with the *Locarno* Treaty (1925) and to secure his country's entry to the *League of Nations* (1920–45) in 1926.
- By supporting the *Dawes Plan* (1924) and introducing the *Rentenmark,* Stresemann led Germany out of economic crisis. Furthermore, he negotiated a reduction in *reparations* payments through the *Young Plan* (1929) and was instrumental in the Allied evacuation from the *Ruhr*.

TIP

Stresemann contributed to the post-1923 recovery of Germany. His death in 1929 coincided disastrously with the start of the *Depression*.

Sudetenland: the western Czechoslovakian area that bordered Germany in 1938 and was inhabited by some 3 million German-speaking people.

- The Treaty of *Saint-Germain* (1920) removed these people from Austria–Hungary and assigned them to Czechoslovakia, which combined with the existence of rich natural resources to make occupation of the Sudetenland an early priority for *Hitler*.
- The Munich Agreement (1938) transferred the Sudetenland to German control and deprived the Czechs of their main lines of defence against German aggression.

TIP An understanding of Sudetenland's fate is essential to explaining *appeasement.*

Suez Crisis, 1956: an international crisis that resulted from the Egyptian government's decision to nationalise (take over) the Suez Canal, which was owned by a British and French company.

- A brief and intense war pitted the Egyptians against France, Britain and Israel. The fighting temporarily closed the canal.
- The US and USSR both condemned the military campaign against Egypt and the *United Nations* ordered Britain and France to withdraw.

TIP Soviet support for Egypt drew the two countries closer together. Egypt's defiance of two former imperial powers enabled *Nasser*, the Egyptian dictator, to emerge as leader of the Arab world.

DS **suffragettes:** women who were prepared to take extreme measures to secure voting rights, or suffrage, for British women.

- In 1903 Emmeline *Pankhurst* formed the Women's Social and Political Union. From 1906 to 1914, its members undertook increasingly aggressive action to advance their cause.
- Faced with government resistance, suffragettes turned to violence. In 1913 Emily Davidson was killed when she threw herself in front of the king's horse at a race.
- The suffragettes called off their campaign in 1914 and made a tremendous contribution to victory in the *Great War* (1914–18).
- Women over the age of 30 were enfranchised (given the right to vote) in 1918 by the *Representation of the People Act*. Ten years later, the vote was extended to women aged over 21.

TIP The suffragette movement was a vital part of the struggle for equal rights for women during the twentieth century.

DS **Sun Yat Sen:** a Chinese revolutionary who formed the *Guomindang* and tried to unite the provinces of China.

- In 1898 Sun Yat Sen set out his three principles for the future of the Chinese nation — *nationalism, democracy* and *socialism*. In 1924 he persuaded the Guomindang to accept communist members.
- When Sun Yat Sen died in 1925, the struggle to succeed him began between his followers (led by *Chiang*) and the Chinese communists (led by Mao *Zedong*).

TIP Sun Yat Sen's successful nationalist revolution in 1911 ended the rule of emperors in China but achieved little else.

superpower: the name given to an extremely powerful nation.

- The term superpower is synonymous with post-1945 USA and *Soviet Union*. The former's immense wealth and the latter's vast territory set them apart in world leadership from all other states struggling to recover from the devastation caused by the *Second World War* (1939–45).

- With the collapse of the Soviet Union in 1991, the US is the only remaining superpower.

DS **Supreme Court:** the highest court in the United States.

- The Supreme Court comprises nine judges whom the president of the USA — with the consent of the Senate in *Congress* — appoints for life.
- The court hears legal appeals and must decide whether laws or policies conflict with the US Constitution.

Syngman Rhee: the leader of South Korea during the *Korean War* (1950–53).

- Syngman Rhee governed through a democracy of sorts, but his rule was marked by corruption and mismanagement.
- He was overthrown after a military coup in 1960.

Tannenburg, Battle of, 1914: a German victory on the Eastern Front that ended the first and only Russian invasion of German territory during the *Great War* (1914–18).

- Two Russian armies were encircled by German troops commanded by General *Hindenburg* and General *Ludendorff*.
- German success at Tannenburg was quickly followed by a second Russian defeat at the Battle of the Masurian Lakes.

TIP The heavy Russian casualties suffered during these battles set the tone for high losses throughout the war. *Nicholas II's* reputation fell after he took personal command of the Russian armed forces in 1915.

tariff: a tax imposed on foreign manufactured goods.

- Tariffs are an integral part of a protectionist economic policy that seeks to give domestically produced goods an advantage.
- Foreign goods are made more expensive and, therefore, less attractive to consumers.
- Tariffs — the opposite of free trade — often result in retaliation and, ultimately, trade wars.

Tehran Conference, 1943: the first wartime meeting as a group of the *Big Three* (*Stalin, Churchill* and *Roosevelt*).

- Churchill and Roosevelt agreed to Stalin's demand for a second military front in France which, it was decided, should be opened in the early summer of 1944.
- Postwar Russian territory would be extended west at the expense of the Poles who would, in turn, be compensated with confiscated German land.
- The need for a postwar peace-keeping organisation was discussed and Stalin declared that the USSR would enter the war against Japan when Germany was defeated.

TIP The meeting was called to repair the increasingly strained wartime alliance. Roosevelt's attempt to achieve reconciliation through personal diplomacy worked with Stalin, but Churchill continued to distrust the Soviet leader.

DS **Tennessee Valley Authority (TVA), 1933:** one of the earliest achievements of the *New Deal*.

- The TVA built dams in the economically depressed Tennessee River Valley to control floods and to generate hydroelectric power.
- The project succeeded in its goal of improving the local economy. There was, however, a cost: soil erosion and pollution were environmentally disastrous byproducts.

TIP The TVA set the pace for intense federal action during the *first hundred days* of the *Roosevelt* administration.

terrorism: the use by minority groups of organised violence to secure political ends.

- Terrorism became increasingly common throughout the world during the second half of the twentieth century.
- Typical terrorist tactics include random bombing, assassination, hijacking, and hostage taking.
- Terrorism can be used by one government against another, or by a group wanting to put pressure on a government. *Authoritarian* governments also use terrorism to crush opposition to their policies.

TIP Use of the term is influenced by personal opinion. As the saying goes: 'One man's terrorist is another man's freedom fighter.'

Tet Offensive, 1968: a *Vietcong* and North Vietnamese offensive across the southern half of the country during the *Vietnam War* (1946–75).

- Communist soldiers temporarily occupied provincial capitals throughout the South, and even the US embassy in Saigon.
- The offensive shocked US public opinion. Up to that point, the US people had been told the war was being won; despite US military power, millions of dollars, and half a million troops the Vietcong could not be defeated.
- Tet was the decisive event that pushed *Johnson* into announcing he would not run again for the presidency.

TIP It was a major turning point in the war. Johnson was advised that the war could not be won, even if the 200,000 more soldiers requested by the army were sent to Vietnam. Peace talks began only a few months after the defeat of the offensive.

DS **Thatcher, Margaret:** a British Conservative who was the country's first woman prime minister (1979–90) and the first since the early nineteenth century to win three successive general elections.

- Thatcher served as secretary of state for education and science (1970–74) before being elected leader of the Conservative Party in 1975.
- A strong ally of *Reagan* during the *Cold War* (1945–91), she took a hard line when dealing with the *Soviet Union*.

- In 1982 Thatcher sent British troops to retake the Falkland Islands from its Argentine invaders.
- Thatcher's domestic policies centred on privatisation of major state industries, battling the *trade union* movement and seeking an agreement with the Irish government over the future of *Ulster*.

DS **Third Reich:** the official name given by the Nazis to their government in Germany between 1933 and 1945, which *Hitler* claimed would last a thousand years.

- The Nazis claimed that the First Reich existed during the Middle Ages and the Second Reich was the period from the unification of Germany in 1871 to defeat in the *Great War* (1914–18).

Third World: countries that are not among the developed capitalist countries (the First World) nor part of the developed former communist, or Second, world.

- Third World countries tend to be the developing nations in Latin America, Africa, and Asia. Many have a colonial past.

DS **Tiananmen Square:** the scene of a brutal 1989 crackdown in Beijing against student demonstrators calling for democratic reform in China.

- Inspired by *Gorbachev's* policies of *glasnost* and *perestroika*, tens of thousands of students packed the square armed only with a list of grievances about inflation, crime, official corruption and the Communist Party's monopoly on power.
- Hundreds of these unarmed students were killed by the Chinese army. US officials condemned the killings, but took no further action. US leaders held that global security and trade needs required friendly Sino-American relations.

TIP

The massacre showed that China's leaders would not allow their authority to be challenged.

Tito, Josip: the communist leader of Yugoslavia who ruled as prime minister (1945–53) and president (1953–80).

- Tito led communist *guerrilla* fighters against German and Italian occupation between 1941 and 1945.
- Determined to protect Yugoslav *sovereignty* and independence, he resisted *Stalin's* attempts to make Yugoslavia a *satellite* of the *Soviet Union*. Yugoslavia was expelled from *Cominform* in 1948.
- Tito is most remembered for his support of the non-aligned movement of countries that wanted to be allies of neither the US nor the USSR.

TIP

Tito maintained a republic made up of many different ethnic and religious groups. When he died in 1980, Yugoslavia began to break up into warring states.

Tonkin Gulf Resolution, 1964: the decision by the US *Congress* authorising President *Johnson* to deploy US forces in Vietnam.

- The resolution followed an alleged clash between US and North Vietnamese naval vessels in international waters off the coast of North Vietnam.
- Johnson persuaded Congress effectively to give him the power to go to war without first consulting it or the US people.

- Johnson used the resolution to launch Operation Rolling Thunder (the bombing of North Vietnam) and to commit US ground troops in increasing numbers to fight alongside the South Vietnamese.

TIP In passing the Tonkin Gulf Resolution, Congress essentially surrendered its powers in the *foreign policy* decision-making process.

totalitarian: a state that has a one-party political system and maintains absolute, or total, power over the individual.

- Examples of twentieth-century totalitarian states are Nazi Germany, fascist Italy and the *Soviet Union*. Rule is typically by a dictator.

total war: a type of warfare that considers the civilian and non-combatant populations as a vital part of the war effort.

- Total war requires the complete mobilisation and involvement of society as part of the war effort.
- This warfare is typically unrestricted and results in heavy civilian loss of life and damage to populated areas.
- Such warfare was not fully waged until the *Second World War* (1939–45), during which some 67% of casualties were civilian.

trade union: an association of workers formed to protect the interests of its members in relations with employers.

- The main goal of a trade union is to use collective bargaining to gain fair wages and safe working conditions in factories and mines.
- In 1900 trade unions founded the British *Labour Party* and are still influential in shaping the party's policies.

trench warfare: the type of fighting that was a dominant military feature of the *Great War* (1914–18).

- Trench warfare started following the failure of the *Schlieffen Plan*, when both sides dug trenches to protect their positions from attack.
- Trenches stretched over 600 kilometres from the Belgian coast to Switzerland in a line known as the *Western Front*.
- Four years of fighting resulted in heavy casualties, as each side tried without success to push the other back.
- Conditions in the trenches were generally poor; soldiers often had to deal with rain, mud, rats, and lack of sleep.
- The area that separated the opposing trench lines was *no-man's land*; in many places it was too dangerous to step here in daylight for the 4 years of the conflict.

TIP An understanding of trench warfare is essential to explaining the military situation during the Great War.

Trianon, Treaty of, 1920: the peace agreement between Hungary and the Allies after the *Great War* (1914–18).

- Hungary lost two-thirds of its pre-war territory, while Czechoslovakia, Romania, Yugoslavia, Italy, and Poland gained land at the expense of the Hungarians.

- In addition to being made liable for *reparations* payments, Hungary's army was limited to 35,000 men.

TIP So great was resentment of this treaty that attempts to revise it dominated Hungarian *foreign policy* between the wars.

Tripartite Pact, 1940: an alliance between Germany, Italy and Japan in which each country agreed to assist the others if one of them was attacked by any new enemy not already in the *Second World War* (1939–45).

- The Germans and Japanese chiefly had the US in mind as the possible enemy of the future.
- In an attempt to secure German protection against the threat of Soviet aggression, Slovakia, Hungary and Romania also joined the pact.

TIP Three days after the Japanese attack on *Pearl Harbor*, *Hitler* honoured the pact by declaring war against the US. Historians agree that this was his biggest diplomatic blunder.

Triple Alliance: see *Alliance system*.

Triple Entente: see *Alliance system*.

DS **Trotsky, Leon:** a Russian revolutionary.

- Trotsky organised the first *soviet* in *Petrograd* and played a key role in the Bolshevik seizure of power during the *October Revolution* (1917).
- As first commissar for foreign affairs, Trotsky represented *Lenin* at the Treaty of *Brest–Litovsk* (1918).
- During the Russian Civil War (1918–21), Trotsky was appointed commissar for war and created the *Red Army*.
- After Lenin's death, *Stalin* undermined Trotsky's position. In 1925 he was expelled from the party and deported soon after. Stalinist agents in Mexico murdered Trotsky in 1940.

TIP Trotsky turned the Red Army into an effective fighting force. His military leadership and organisational skills were key factors in the Bolshevik victory over the *White Russians*.

DS **Truman, Harry:** the US Democratic president (1945–53) whose administration was dominated by the *Cold War* (1945–91).

- Following the sudden death of Roosevelt, President Truman authorised the use of the *atomic bomb* against Japan.
- He announced his *Truman Doctrine* (1947) and *Marshall Aid* (1947). His refusal to give in to Stalin led to the *Berlin Airlift* (1948–49) and his determination to halt communist expansion convinced him to send US troops to fight in the *Korean War* (1950–53).
- Truman's Fair Deal domestic reform programme sought to benefit workers, farmers, the retired, African–Americans and people in need of health care.

TIP

Truman was unpopular when he left office. The fact that he strengthened presidential power and provided much of the foundation of US prosperity in the 1960s has enhanced his reputation.

Truman Doctrine, 1947: *Truman's* policy pledging US support of free peoples who were resisting communist interference from inside or from outside their nation.

- The doctrine helped launch *containment*, the idea that the US had to make a stand against communism everywhere.
- The doctrine was first put to the test during the Greek Civil War in early 1947, when US money and military advisers helped the Greek government to crush communist rebels.
- US involvement in the *Berlin Airlift* (1948–49) and the *Korean War* (1950–53) was a direct result of the Truman Doctrine.

TIP

Stalin condemned the Truman Doctrine as an attempt to encircle and isolate the *Soviet Union*.

DS **TVA:** see *Tennessee Valley Authority*.

U2 incident: see *Powers.*

U-boats: German submarines used during the *Great War* (1914–18) and the *Second World War* (1939–45).

- U-boats sank hundreds of ships travelling to and from Britain and its allies. The pressure they placed on Britain was tremendous; mass starvation became a real issue in 1917.
- During the first 2 years of the Second World War, supplies of vital goods and war material were heavily disrupted.
- The Battle of the *Atlantic* witnessed the heaviest use of U-boats between 1940 and 1945.

DS **Ulster:** the six northern counties of Ireland that are part of the United Kingdom. Also known as Northern Ireland.

- Ulster's protestant majority population is descended from migrants from Scotland and England.
- On the eve of the *Great War* (1914–18), the issue of Home Rule pushed Ulster to the brink of civil war.
- The Government of Ireland Act (1920) paved the way for the establishment of the Irish Free State and Ulster. Between 1921 and 1972, Ulster enjoyed limited self-government.
- The Troubles — which involved British forces, Ulster Loyalists and the *Irish Republican Army* — broke out in 1969.

TIP

Ulster was a significant issue in domestic British politics during the twentieth century.

UN: see *United Nations.*

unification: the process of uniting, or joining together, states or parts of divided nations.

- Unification usually takes place to bring about economic, political, or military benefits.
- The joining together of East and West Germany in 1991 after some 50 years of division is an example of reunification.

United Nations: an international organisation set up in 1945 by delegates from 50 nations to succeed the *League of Nations* (1920–45).

- The UN's main aim is to preserve peace but its work includes preventing disease, improving education and protecting refugees.
- The permanent members of the Security Council (the US, Britain, Russia, France and China) have the authority to ensure international peace.
- The UN has the power to impose *sanctions* and the right to call on member states to provide troops for peacekeeping operations.
- UN agencies, like the World Health Organisation and the Food and Agricultural Organisation, have done much to help needy people around the world.
- At the time of its fifty-fifth anniversary (2000), 185 nations belonged to the United Nations.

TIP

The United Nations has found it easier to establish and maintain peace following international conflict than it has to prevent the outbreak of war.

DS **USSR:** see *Soviet Union.*

VC: see *Vietcong*.

Verdun, Battle of, 1916: a German attack on French positions in an attempt to break the stalemate on the *Western Front* during the *Great War* (1914–18).

- The German commander, Falkenhayn, said he wanted to 'bleed the French white' by drawing their reserves into a 15-mile sector around the city of Verdun.
- During a 300-day battle, the French prevented the Germans from capturing Verdun. The French lost over 400,000 men, the Germans nearly 350,000.

TIP

Verdun was the only Great War battle in which the defenders lost more men than the attackers. Its effect on the French continued long after 1918 and contributed to the French military collapse at the beginning of the *Second World War*.

Versailles, Treaty of, 1919: the peace agreement between Germany and the Allies after the *Great War* (1914–18).

- Article 231 of the treaty declared Germany's responsibility for causing the war and the subsequent damage and cost, human and otherwise; the amount of *reparations* payments was set at £6,600 million.
- Poland, Czechoslovakia, France and Belgium all gained land at Germany's expense. Its overseas empire was broken up and shared between the victors and the *Anschluss* was forbidden.
- A demilitarised zone was established in the *Rhineland* on the Franco-German border and the German army limited to 100,000 men.

TIP

An understanding of the Treaty of Versailles is essential, particularly how German resentment towards it helped undermine German democracy and assisted the rise of *Hitler*.

Vichy France, 1940–44: the area of France controlled by a pro-German government following the defeat of France in the *Second World War* (1939–45).

- The Franco-German armistice gave Germany the western coast and northern France. The remainder was put under the control of a right-wing government based in the town of Vichy.

- The Vichy was anti-republican and believed in 'order, authority, and patriotism'. Its anti-Semitic laws sent thousands of French Jews and others to their deaths in Nazi Germany.
- Because *Hitler* distrusted Vichy politicians, he ordered the occupation of the whole of France in 1942. The Vichy government collapsed 2 years later following the *D-Day* landings in northern France.

TIP The Free French, under the future French leader Charles de Gaulle, set up an alternative to Vichy collaboration in London.

Vietcong: communist fighters who waged *guerrilla warfare* against US and South Vietnamese forces during the *Vietnam War* (1946–75).

- The organisation was the military wing of the National Liberation Front (NLF), set up in 1960 by *Ho Chi Minh* to overthrow President *Diem* and unite North and South Vietnam.
- During the *Tet offensive* (1968), the Vietcong launched attacks throughout South Vietnam. Although thousands of its fighters were killed and the offensive crushed, the Vietcong won a propaganda victory that turned US public opinion against the war.

TIP The rapid growth in Vietcong numbers in the early 1960s and the inability of South Vietnamese forces to defeat them contributed to the US government's decision to send increasing numbers of combat troops to Vietnam.

Vietminh: the Vietnamese resistance movement founded in 1941 by *Ho Chi Minh* to fight the Japanese occupation.

- The Vietminh accepted members with many political opinions, but was dominated by communists.
- Following the defeat of Japan (1945), Vietminh forces fought a war of independence against the French from 1946 to 1954.
- The *Geneva Accords* of 1954 created the independent communist state of North Vietnam.

TIP After 1960, the Vietminh provided the core of the National Liberation Front that wanted a united Vietnam.

Vietnamisation: *Nixon's* policy of withdrawing US forces from Vietnam.

- Vietnamisation was part of the Nixon Doctrine, which stated that the US would help those nations 'that help themselves'.
- From 1969, the US transferred weapons, arms and equipment to South Vietnamese forces so the pro-US government would steadily take over all civil and military aspects of the war.
- In January 1973 Nixon signed a peace agreement with North Vietnam that included a promise to withdraw all remaining US troops from Vietnam within 60 days. The South Vietnamese government collapsed 2 years later.

While anti-war demonstrations intensified in the US, elements of the military tried to convince Nixon that they could win a decisive victory in Vietnam.

Vietnam War, 1946–75: the conflict fought to establish an independent, communist-controlled state in Vietnam.

- From 1946 to 1954, the *Vietminh* fought a war of independence against French occupation. Following the French defeat at Dien Bien Phu, Vietnam won its independence and was divided into North and South by the *Geneva Accords* (1954).
- *Vietminh* and *Vietcong* fighters battled South Vietnamese and US troops from 1956 to 1964. Large-scale US intervention began in 1964 following the *Tonkin Gulf Resolution*.
- The years 1965–73 witnessed a US military build-up, with air raids against North Vietnam and both conventional and *guerrilla warfare* campaigns.
- The war ended in 1975 when the North invaded and overran the South. The country was reunited under communist rule and the US suffered a military defeat that undermined its policy of *containment*.

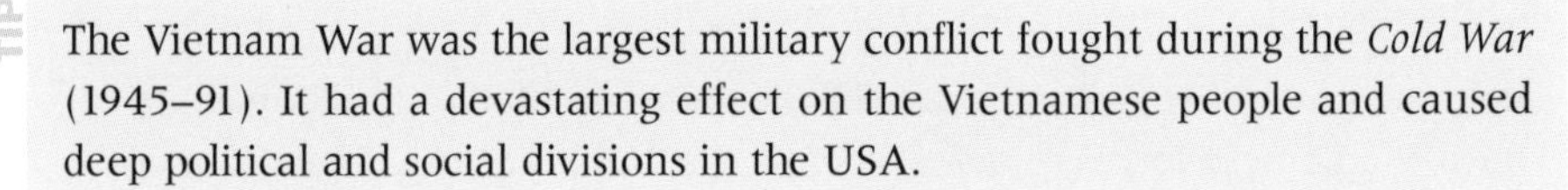

The Vietnam War was the largest military conflict fought during the *Cold War* (1945–91). It had a devastating effect on the Vietnamese people and caused deep political and social divisions in the USA.

DS **Wagner Act, 1935:** trade union and industrial relations legislation that was one of the first measures of the *New Deal.*

- US workers were granted the right to set up trade unions and to bargain collectively with industrial management.
- Employers were prevented from persecuting or punishing workers who wanted to join a union.
- The act created the National Labor Relations Board to ensure democratic union elections and to penalise unfair practices by employers.

TIP The Wagner Act gave workers' unions federal recognition for the first time and was a turning point in US industrial relations.

Wall Street Crash, 1929: the sudden collapse of the New York stock exchange in Wall Street led to an economic *Depression* throughout the US and the rest of the world.

- The crash put an end to the *boom* the US had enjoyed throughout the 1920s.
- Between 24 and 29 October a panic on the stock market caused banks to fail, businesses to collapse and unemployment to rise dramatically.
- US companies reacted by withdrawing overseas investments, which had global repercussions.

TIP While the Wall Street Crash was an important feature of the interwar economic crisis, it in itself did not cause the Depression. Rather, it highlighted the already weak state of the world economy.

DS **Wannsee Conference, 1942:** a meeting of senior Nazi officials in a Berlin suburb that formalised the *Final Solution.*

- The conference was led by Reinhard Heydrich and set in motion the transportation of European Jewry in German-occupied territory to *death camps.* A key role was assigned to *Eichmann.*
- Representatives from the main Nazi ministries, including the German Foreign Office, and the Race and Resettlement Office, attended.

- Mass killings by the *Einsatzgruppen* had been going on for some time before the conference was convened.

TIP

An understanding of the Wannsee Conference is essential to explain the Nazi transition from random murder to systematic extermination.

DS **war communism:** the Bolshevik control of industry and food supplies during the Russian Civil War.

- War communism involved centralised management of factories, mines, workshops and railways and forbade private trading.
- Grain was seized from the peasants to feed Bolshevik soldiers and workers in the cities.
- By 1921, it was clear that war communism was a failure, despite the Bolshevik victory over the *White Russians*. Industrial output fell sharply and severe famine hit the Russian countryside.

TIP

The *Kronstadt Mutiny* (1921), together with the shortage of basic goods, forced *Lenin* to replace war communism with the *New Economic Policy*.

War Guilt clause: article 231 of the Treaty of *Versailles* (1919), which forced Germany to accept responsibility for causing the outbreak of the *Great War* (1914–18).

- Article 231 allowed the Allies to make Germany liable for high *reparations* payments.
- An outraged German people felt powerless to do anything until *Hitler* promised to overturn article 231.

TIP

An understanding of the impact of the clause is essential to explaining German opposition to Versailles and Hitler's rise to power.

Warsaw Pact, 1955: a military alliance between the *Soviet Union* and its East European *satellite* states that was the counterpart to NATO.

- The pact was set up following West Germany's entry into NATO. The original member states were Albania, Bulgaria, Czechoslovakia, East Germany, Hungary, Poland, Romania and the USSR.
- In addition to establishing an agreement on mutual defence against any threatened attack, member states pledged to respect each other's independence and sovereignty through non-intervention.
- Despite this, Moscow increasingly used the Warsaw Pact to control its communist neighbours; in 1968, Warsaw Pact troops were sent into Czechoslovakia to crush the *Prague Spring*.

TIP

The Warsaw Pact was one of the two military alliances that divided Europe into two armed camps for over 35 years. In that time each remained on constant alert.

Washington Conference, 1921–22: an international meeting to discuss naval disarmament and the Far East.

- Britain, France, Italy, Portugal, Belgium, Holland, Japan, China and the US were represented.
- The conference resulted in the strengthening of Sino-Japanese relations and an agreement by the powers not to build any major warships for 10 years.
- Britain, the US and Japan established a ratio of 5:5:3 between them for battleships.

TIP At the time, the conference seemed to mark a substantial step towards peace through arms control.

DS **Watergate Affair:** the fallout from an incident that took place during the 1972 US presidential election that forced *Nixon* to resign.

- Watergate began with the arrest of several burglars in the Washington DC headquarters of the *Democratic Party*. The arrested men were employed by Nixon's re-election organisation.
- Nixon evidently authorised the break-in and started a cover-up to obstruct justice.
- It emerged that Nixon possessed tape-recorded conversations about the incident. He agreed to hand these over to the appropriate authorities only after being forced to by the *Supreme Court*.
- The US senate voted to impeach (dismiss) Nixon, but he resigned before any action could be taken against him.

TIP The Watergate scandal forced the US people to accept that their president was a crook. It also resulted in *Congress* passing several laws to restrict the power of the presidency.

DS **Weimar Republic, 1918–33:** the 1918–33 German Federal Republic, established following the abdication of Kaiser *William II*.

- The Weimar constitution provided for a 7-year presidential office, *proportional representation*, and guaranteed federal rights.
- From the beginning, the Weimar had few friends and many enemies. The challenges and obstacles it faced included the burden of *reparations*, a financial collapse in 1922–23, and uprisings by the communists and the Nazis.
- Under the leadership of *Stresemann*, Germany enjoyed a period of recovery secured by the *Dawes Plan* (1924) and the *Young Plan* (1929). The Weimar could not, however, survive the *Depression* and came to an end with the appointment of *Hitler* as German chancellor in January 1933.

DS **welfare state:** the main domestic achievement of the Labour government elected into office in 1945.

- *Attlee* carried out the proposals highlighted in the *Beveridge Report* (1942), by which the government took on primary responsibility for safeguarding the social and economic well-being of the population.
- Its main features are the National Health Service, which provides free health care for all, and the National Insurance Act (1946), which provides pensions

for all working women from the age of 60 and men from 65. This is financed by contributions from both workers and employers.

TIP The creation of the welfare state is one of the most important domestic developments in twentieth-century British history.

DS **West Bank:** the agriculturally rich territory to the west of the River Jordan, that was part of Jordan until 1967 when it was occupied by Israel during the second *Arab–Israeli War.*

- After its victory in the *Six-Day War*, the Israeli government ordered the army to confiscate Arab land in the West Bank and to build Jewish settlements there to make a buffer zone between Israel and its enemies.
- In doing so, Israel ignored *United Nations* demands that it immediately withdraw from the area.
- The 1978 *Camp David Agreement* provided for greater Palestinian self-rule in the West Bank. It took another 15 years and the 1993 Israeli–Palestinian peace agreement before this started to happen.

TIP Ongoing disagreement over the future of the West Bank remains a major obstacle to a lasting peace between Israel and the Palestinians.

Western Front: the largely static line of battle in Western Europe during the *Great War* (1914–18).

- The Western Front was a line of trenches that stretched form the Belgian coast to Switzerland.
- Each side suffered heavy casualties trying to move the other back. The most notable examples were the Battles of the *Somme* (1916) and *Verdun* (1916), and the third Battle of *Ypres* (1917).

DS **White Russians:** the collective enemies of the Bolsheviks after 1918.

- Bolshevik enemies included supporters of the tsar, landowners, tsarist generals and groups such as the *Mensheviks* and Social Revolutionaries with whom *Lenin* refused to share power.
- The White Russians hated the Bolsheviks, or Reds, because they were hostile to religion and because they seized land, property and businesses of the wealthy.
- Supported by British, French, US and Japanese forces, the Whites fought the Reds during the Russian Civil War (1918–21). The conflict saw bitter fighting, and atrocities committed by both sides — not least the *Cheka* — before the Whites were defeated.

DS **William II:** the German emperor (1888–1918) who led Germany into the *Great War* (1914–18) and was forced to abdicate following defeat.

- William II was Queen Victoria's grandson and King George VI's cousin.
- His strict military education and pride in German sea power led him to believe in Germany's role as a world leader.
- Although he wanted to limit Germany to a one-front war, he supported the *Schlieffen Plan* and the German generals' decision to go to war in 1914.

- Between 1918 and 1941, he lived out his life in Holland.

TIP William's determination to rule as well as reign meant he was an important figure in causing the Great War.

DS **Wilson, Woodrow:** the US Democratic president (1913–21) who led his country to victory in the *Great War* (1914–18) and played a key role in the *Paris Peace Conference* (1919–20).

- Wilson pursued *neutrality* in the conflict and won the 1916 presidential election on the slogan 'He Kept Us Out of War'. German *U-boat* attacks on US shipping and the *Zimmerman Telegram* (1917) persuaded him to declare war in 1917.
- Wilson's *Fourteen Points* were the basis for the post-1918 peace. These emphasised the need for a *League of Nations* to be set up.
- Pressured by the vengefulness of the French leader *Clemenceau* and — to a lesser extent — the British prime minister, *Lloyd George,* Wilson had to accept compromise at Paris.
- The US Senate refused to ratify (support) the Treaty of *Versailles* (1919). While travelling around the USA in 1920, Wilson suffered a stroke and failed to win support for his ideas.

TIP An understanding of Wilson's ideas is essential to explaining the peace settlement that followed the Great War.

DS **Witte, Sergei:** the Russian finance minister (1892–1903) and prime minister (1905–06).

- Witte believed the key to Russia's future lay in industrialisation. He raised French loans and used his control over commerce, industry and labour relations to assist construction of the Trans-Siberian Railway.
- In 1903 he was dismissed by *Nicholas II* but then recalled to negotiate an end to the Russo-Japanese War (1905–06).
- Following the *Revolution of 1905,* Witte issued the *October Manifesto*. He was again sacked in 1906 and replaced by *Stolypin*.

TIP Witte played a key role in the early stages of the modernisation of Russia as well as in helping the tsar remain in power following the Revolution of 1905.

DS **Works Progress Administration (WPA), 1935:** an organisation that created public works programmes during the *New Deal*.

- The WPA was set up by the Emergency Relief Appropriation Act (1935) and headed by Harry Hopkins.
- By the time it was abolished in 1943, the WPA had provided employment for more than 8.5 million people and built more than 650,000 miles of roads, 125,000 public buildings and 8,000 parks.
- What was important to Hopkins was that the unemployed were returned to work. Exactly what type of work they did was a lesser priority; artists, authors and actors were employed by the WPA at one time or another.

TIP

During its time, the WPA was the country's biggest single employer, giving work to an average of 2 million Americans each year.

WPA: see *Works Progress Administration.*

DS **X, Malcolm:** an African–American political activist and chief spokesman for the Black Muslims, or Nation of Islam, a small radical group that wanted separatism from whites.

- Malcolm X was a one-time criminal who converted to Islam while imprisoned.
- When Martin Luther *King* was preaching non-violence, Malcolm X urged African–Americans to seize their freedom 'by any means necessary'.
- In early 1965, gunmen from the Black Muslims — who believed Malcolm X had betrayed their leader Elijah Muhammad and their cause by expressing cautious support for the non-violent civil rights movement — murdered him.

TIP For both blacks and whites, Malcolm X's militant position symbolised black defiance and self-respect.

Yalta Conference, 1945: a wartime meeting of *Churchill, Roosevelt* and *Stalin* to discuss policy towards Europe following victory in the *Second World War* (1939–45).

- Churchill, Roosevelt and Stalin each arrived at Yalta with his own agenda; the outcome was a series of trade-offs and compromises.
- The future of Poland was a sticking point. The three men reached an agreement that favoured the *Soviet Union*. Given that it was occupied by the *Red Army* there was little alternative.
- Germany was to be divided into four zones, the fourth zone to be administered by France. The same was to true of Berlin.
- The question of *reparations* was discussed. Stalin wanted a precise figure, but the two Western allies insisted on determining Germany's ability to pay.
- It was agreed that an Allied committee would consider the sum of $20 billion as a starting point for further discussion.

TIP This conference was the high point in the wartime alliance as each leader came away with something he wanted. However, suspicion grew and by the time of the *Potsdam* meeting a few months later, conditions had been created for future *Cold War* (1945–91).

DS **Yeltsin, Boris:** president of the Russian Federation (1991–99).

- Yeltsin rose to national prominence as a leading figure in the defeat of the attempted 1991 coup by hard-line communists against *Gorbachev*. He succeeded Gorbachev following the collapse of the *Soviet Union* in 1991.
- To solve Russia's economic problems, Yeltsin moved the country to a market economy. In 1999 he stepped aside in the face of growing opposition to his policies and because of his own poor health. Vladimir Putin succeeded him.

TIP Yeltsin is an important figure in the collapse of the USSR and the end of the *Cold War* (1945–91).

DS **Yom-Kippur War, 1973:** see *Arab–Israeli Wars*.

Young Plan, 1929: an attempt to restructure German *reparations* payments.

- The plan aimed to address the fact that Germany had not made any payments since 1921.
- The cost of reparations was reduced to the figure of 34,500 gold marks and the payments were spread out over a period lasting until 1988.
- The world financial crisis prevented Germany from making any payments in 1931–32. When *Hitler* came to power in 1933 he halted all reparations payments.

TIP Various factors — the death of *Stresemann*, the *Depression* and the rise of *National Socialism* — all meant that the Young Plan never actually came into operation.

Ypres, Battles of, 1914, 1915, 1917: three major battles fought for control of the strategically important Belgian town of Ypres during the *Great War* (1914–18).

- The town was in the British sector of the *Western Front* and continuous fighting took place around it for 4 years.
- The battles are most remembered for the heavy casualties inflicted on both sides, the terrible living and fighting conditions experienced by the soldiers who fought there, and the first use of poison gas in war, by the Germans (1915).
- The Germans came close to the outskirts of Ypres and destroyed the town with almost constant shelling. However, they never captured it.

TIP In a war characterised by scenes of unspeakable horror, Ypres was undoubtedly one of the worst and most feared battlefields that any soldier could be sent to.

DS **Zedong, Mao:** the Chinese Communist Party founder (1921) and leader of the People's Republic of China (1949–1976).

- Mao introduced a brand of communism developed from Marxism and the ideas of *Lenin*, which was based on the peasantry and *guerrilla warfare*. This came to be known as 'Maoism'.
- Mao fought against the ruling *Guomindang* and led his supporters on the *Long March* (1934).
- Following victory in the civil war, Mao established a personality cult that contributed to both the *Great Leap Forward* and the *Cultural Revolution*.

TIP A knowledge of the key points of Mao's political life is essential to an understanding of East Asian history.

DS **Zimmerman Telegram, 1917:** a coded message from Arthur Zimmerman, the German foreign minister, to the German embassy in Mexico that contributed to the US decision to enter the *Great War* (1914–18).

- The telegram suggested a German–Mexican alliance and stated that once victory was achieved, Mexico would recover 'lost territory in New Mexico, Texas, and Arizona'.
- The telegram was intercepted by British intelligence and passed to Washington, where it was released to the press.

TIP Anti-German feeling was already running high in the USA because of the *U-boat* campaign; memories of the sinking of the passenger liner *Lusitania* were still fresh. Three months after the telegram was revealed, *Wilson* declared war against Germany.

DS **Zinoviev, Grigorii:** a Bolshevik who is most remembered for allegedly sending a letter to British communists urging them to promote revolution.

- Zinoviev sided with *Stalin* to prevent *Trotsky* from succeeding *Lenin*, but fell victim to Stalin's paranoia and was expelled from the Communist Party in 1927. Nine years later he was condemned during the *Great Terror* and executed.

- The letter he supposedly wrote in 1924 was published in the British press and was taken to show that Labour sympathy towards Russia was encouraging the British communists.
- The *Labour Party* blamed its overwhelming defeat in the 1924 general election on the letter.

TIP

Zinoviev was one of the many original Bolsheviks who helped establish the Soviet Union and was then tried and condemned during the Stalinist era.

DS **Zionism:** the movement for a national homeland for Jews.

- Zionism was launched by Theodore Herzl in the late 1890s as a reaction to rising *anti-Semitism* in Europe.
- Zionists identified *Palestine* as the site to be colonised for the Jewish state. Zion is the Jewish word for Jerusalem.
- The *Balfour Declaration* (1917) was a statement of British support for a Jewish homeland in Palestine. Zionist groups such as the *Stern Gang* and *Irgun* used *terrorism* to help secure the birth of the state of Israel in 1948.